Visitors'
LONDON

WIGMORE COURT

071 935 0928

25 S
40 D

Nicholson

An Imprint of Bartholomew
A Division of HarperCollins*Publishers*

A Nicholson Guide

Nicholson an imprint of
Bartholomew a division of
HarperCollins*Publishers*

First published 1974
9th edition 1992

© Nicholson 1992

London Map
© Nicholson generated from the Bartholomew
London Digital Database

London Underground Map by
permission of London Regional Transport
LRT Registered User No 92/1496

Other maps © Nicholson

Nicholson
HarperCollins*Publishers*
77-85 Fulham Palace Road
Hammersmith
London W6 8JB

Great care has been taken throughout this book to be accurate,
but the publishers cannot accept responsibility for any errors which
appear, or their consequences.

Printed in Great Britain by
Scotprint Ltd, Musselburgh

ISBN 0 7028 1295 1

92/9/1515 BNU

SYMBOLS AND ABBREVIATIONS

A   - Access/Mastercard/Eurocard
Ax - American Express
Dc - Diners Club
V   - Visa/Barclaycard

Average prices for a three-course meal for one
without wine but including VAT:
£   - £10.00 or under
££   - £10.00-£20.00
£££   - £20.00-£30.00
£££+ - £30.00 and over

Reserve - advisable to reserve
B   - breakfast
L   - lunch
D   - dinner
🌓 - open all day 11.00-23.00 Mon-Sat, 12.00-14.00 & 19.00-
       22.30 Sun.
(M) - membership required

Opening times
Many places are closed on Xmas Day, New Year's Day and Good
Friday, and general opening times are subject to change, so it is
always advisable to check first.

CONTENTS

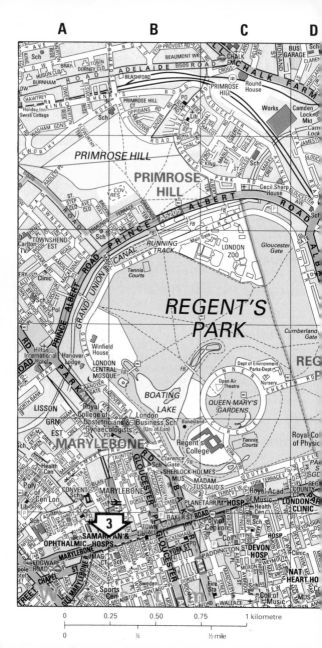

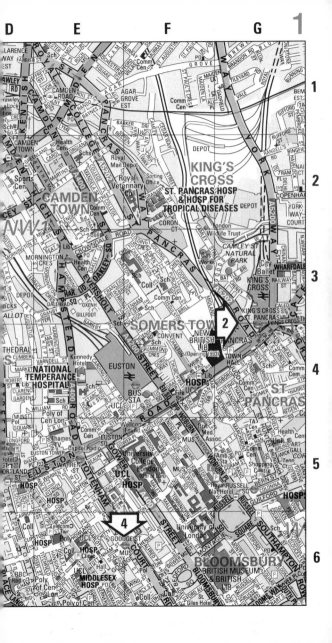

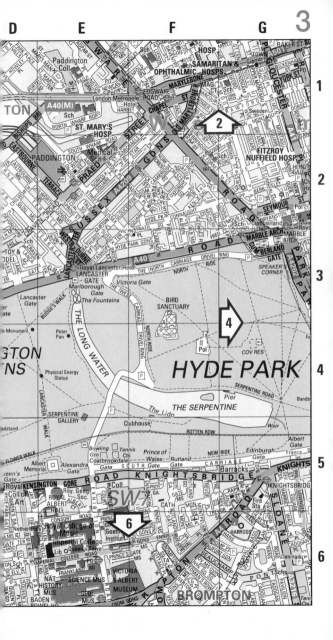

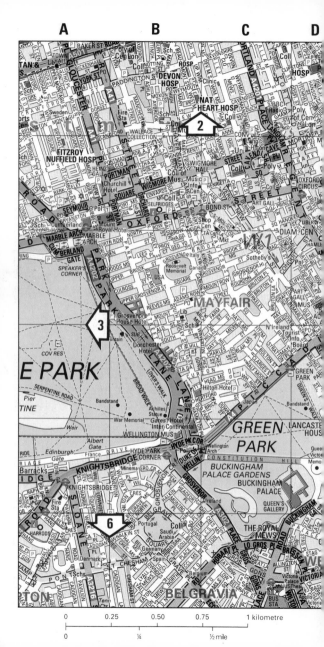

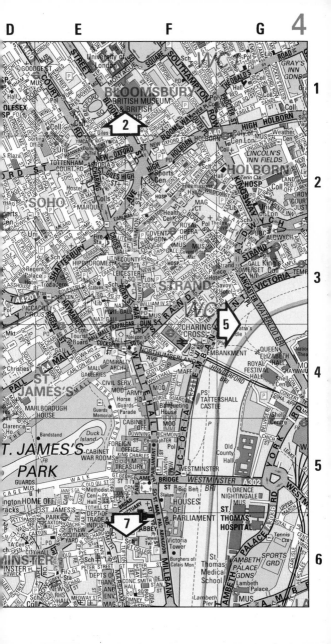

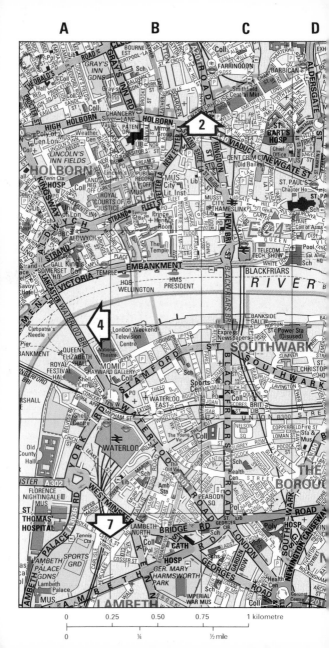

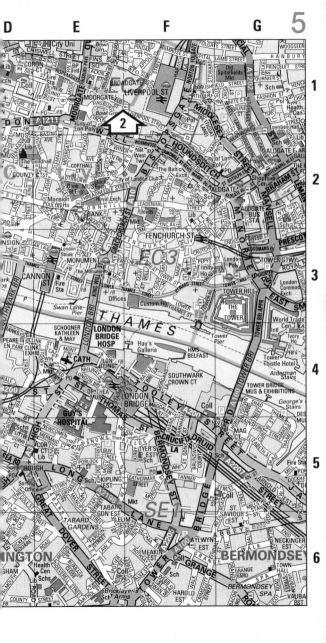

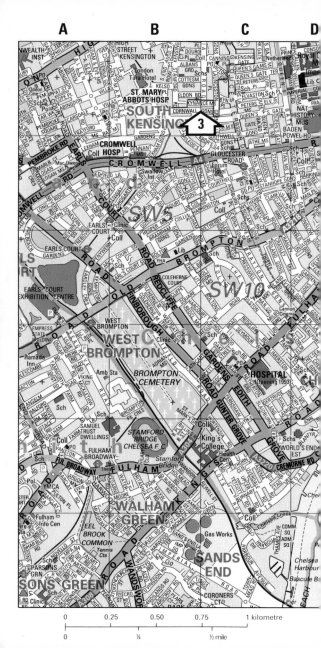

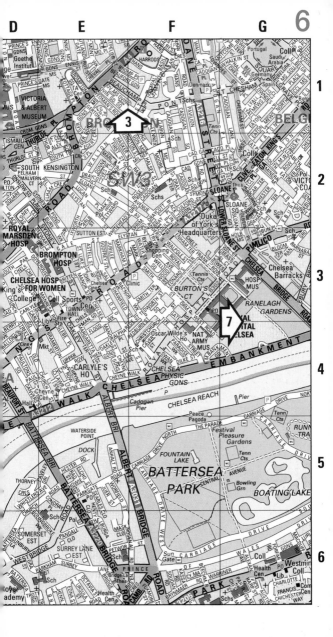

ESSENTIALS ON ARRIVAL

Arriving in London can be daunting, there is so much to take in. However, with essential information at your fingertips, it doesn't have to be an unpleasant experience. Here is useful information you may need from the outset, which will allow you to enjoy all the delights London has to offer.

From airports to the city

Gatwick Airport
Horley, Surrey. (0293) 528822. ***By train***: Gatwick Express (071-928 5100) to Victoria Station (**7 B2**). Trains take *30 mins* and run from *06.20-22.00 (every 15 mins), 22.00-01.00 (every 30 mins), 01.00-06.00 (every hour on the hour) Mon-Sun*. ***By coach***: Flightline 777 (081-668 7261) to Victoria Bus Station (**7 B2**). Coaches take about *75 mins* (longer in heavy traffic) and run from *06.00-23.00 (approx one every hour) Mon-Sun*. ***By car***: M23/A23 to central London, *approx 1 hour*.

Heathrow Airport
Bath Rd, Heathrow, Middx. 081-759 4321. ***By tube***: (Piccadilly line) *approx 50-60 mins* to Piccadilly Circus (**4 E3**) and run from Heathrow *05.08-23.49 Mon-Sat, 06.01-22.43 Sun* and from Piccadilly Circus to Heathrow *05.46-24.21 Mon-Sat, 07.05-23.36 Sun*. ***By bus***: (071-222 1234) A1 to Grosvenor Gdns SW1 (**7 B1**) or A2 to Woburn Pl WC1 (**1 G5**), Euston Bus Station (**1 F4**), Marylebone Rd NW1 (**1 A6**) or Oxford St W1 (**4 C2**). The bus takes about *60-80 mins* (longer in heavy traffic) and runs from *06.00-22.15 (every 20-30 mins) Mon-Sun*. There is another bus service, Flightline 767 (081-668 7261), to Victoria Bus Station (**7 B2**) *06.15-18.30 (every hour) Mon-Sun*. ***By car***: M4 to west London *approx 30 mins*, but can take longer in heavy traffic.

London City Airport
King George V Dock, Silvertown E16. 071-474 5555. Mainly used by businessmen commuting to and from London for meetings. Flights go to Paris, Brussels, Rotterdam, Lille and Jersey. ***By rail***: British Rail from Silvertown to Stratford (Central line underground), then *45-min* journey to central London. ***By boat***: Riverbus from London City Airport Pier, which leaves *approx every hour* and takes about *35 mins*.

Luton Airport
Luton, Beds. (0582) 405100. **By train**: to King's Cross Station (on the Thameslink line) (**1 G3**) trains take about *45 mins* and run from *05.00-08.00 (every 30 mins), 08.00-20.00 (every 10 mins), 20.00-23.30 (every 30 mins), 23.30-05.00 (every hour) Mon-Sun*. Connecting buses take passengers to the airport, but there are no night buses, between *20.00-05.00* passengers must take a taxi. No trains between *01.50-05.00 Sat-Sun*.
By coach: to Victoria Bus Station (**7 B2**) coaches take about *75 mins* and run from *05.30-22.00 (every hour, except 21.00) Mon-Sun (from 06.00 Sat & Sun)*.

Stansted Airport
Stansted, Essex. (0279) 662380. **By train**: to Liverpool Street Station (**2 G6**) from Stansted Station (underneath the airport terminal) the train takes *41 mins* and runs from *06.00-23.00 (every 30 mins) Mon-Sun*. **By coach**: to Victoria (**7 B2**) the coach takes *90 mins* and runs from Stansted *06.40-18.55 (every 2 hours) Mon-Sun* and from Victoria *09.00-21.00 Mon-Sun*.

Hotel booking agents

Accommodation Service of the London Tourist Board   **7 B2**
London Tourist Board Information Centre, Victoria Station Forecourt SW1. 071-730 3488. Information and bookings. *Open 09.00-20.30 Mon-Sun*. Charge.

Concordia Worldwide Hotel Reservations   **7 B1**
53 Grosvenor Gdns SW1. 071-730 9158. All kinds of hotels in London, Britain and worldwide. Sales desk at Victoria Station, opposite Platform 12 (**7 B2**) 071-828 4646. *Open 09.30-17.30 Mon-Fri & 09.30-12.30 Sat*. Charge.

Hotel Booking Service   **4 D3**
Cashmere House, 13-14 Golden Sq W1. 071-437 5052. Knowledgeable service on hotels in London, UK and worldwide. *Open 09.30-17.30 Mon-Fri*. Free.

Hotel Reservations Centre   **7 B2**
10 Buckingham Palace Rd SW1. 071-828 2425. Bookings all over Britain. *Open 09.00-17.00 Mon-Fri*. Free.

Information centres

British Travel Centre   **4 D3**
12 Regent St SW1. 071-730 3400. Home of the British Tourist Authority Information Centre, incorporating a British Rail ticket office and a bureau de change. Details on where to go throughout the UK – book a room, a coach trip or theatre ticket, buy plane or train tickets or hire a car. *Open 09.00-18.30 Mon-Fri, 10.00-16.00 Sat & Sun*.

City of London Information Centre   **5 D2**
St Paul's Churchyard EC4. 071-606 3030. Information and advice with specific reference to the 'Square Mile'. Free leaflets and literature available. *Open May-Sep 09.30-17.00 Mon-Sun; Oct-Apr 09.30-17.00 Mon-Fri, 09.30-12.30 Sat.*

London Tourist Board Information Centre   **7 B2**
Victoria Station Forecourt SW1. 071-730 3488. Travel and tourist information for London and England. Most languages spoken. Hotel reservations, theatre and tour bookings, guide books and maps. *Open Apr-Nov 08.00-20.00 Mon-Sun; Dec-Mar 09.00-19.00 Mon-Sat, 09.00-17.00 Sun. Telephone service 09.00-18.00 Mon-Fri all year.*

Other London Tourist Board information centres at:

Harrods, Knightsbridge SW1   **3 G6**
Heathrow Central Underground Station
Selfridges, 400 Oxford St W1   **4 B2**
Tower of London, West Gate E1   **5 G3**

London Transport Travel Information Centre   **4 E6**
55 Broadway SW1. 071-222 1234. They operate and will answer queries about buses, the underground and Green Line coaches and have general tourist information. There are free maps of the underground and bus routes, and information leaflets in French, German and English. *Opening times vary, phone for details. Automatic telephone call queueing system.*

Other London Transport information centres at the following underground stations:

Euston   **1 F4**
Heathrow
King's Cross   **1 G3**
Oxford Circus   **4 D2**
Piccadilly Circus   **4 E3**
Victoria (British Rail station)   **7 B2**

Scottish Tourist Board   **4 E4**
19 Cockspur St SW1. 071-930 8661. Tourist leaflets and information on mainland Scotland and the islands. *Open 09.00-18.00 Mon-Fri, 10.00-16.00 Sat for leaflets and information (10.00-16.00 Mon-Fri for bookings).*

Wales Tourist Board   **4 C4**
34 Piccadilly W1. 071-409 0969. Leaflets and information for the visitor to Wales. *Open May-Sep 09.00-18.30 Mon-Fri, to 17.30 Sat, 10.00-16.00 Sun; Oct-Apr 09.00-18.30 Mon-Fri, 10.00-16.00 Sat.*

On the move

London has a comprehensive system of public transport with three different services – the bus, the underground (tube) and

British Rail overground trains. It is one of the busiest in Europe, but if you take time to work out your route carefully it can give an excellent dimension on London life.

For the latest update on the travel situation call **Travel Check** *(24hrs) on 071-222 1200.*

The majority of public transport services in London make no provision for disabled passengers. Consult Nicholson's Access in London for advice on getting around.

THE UNDERGROUND

Commonly known as the 'tube', for the visitor to London this is the simplest way of getting around. Very efficient in central London and a good service to north London, although few lines run south of the river, where British Rail offers a more comprehensive service. The tubes run between *approx 05.30-00.15 Mon-Sat, 07.30-23.30 Sun.* All tube stations have a notice showing the times of first and last trains and timetables are issued free at Travel Information Centres. **Fares** are graduated according to zones. Travelcards, giving unlimited travel for one day, a week, a month or a year provide considerable savings. Travelcards can be used on both the underground, DLR and buses, and can be bought at any tube station. Keep some 5p, 10p, 20p and £1 coins handy to use in the ticket machines. Cheap day returns available if you start your journey after *09.30 Mon-Fri* or *any time Sat & Sun.* Keep your ticket to use in the exit machine at your destination. **Smoking** is illegal anywhere on the underground, including in the ticket halls, on stairs, escalators and platforms, as well as in the trains.

Docklands Light Railway (DLR)

This is the newest part of the underground system, opened in 1987 to serve the 'new city' of Docklands. It runs from Tower Gateway, near Tower Hill, to Island Gardens opposite Greenwich on the Isle of Dogs. The red, white and blue trains are computer-operated, although they do have a guard/ticket collector on board. There are excellent views from their high viaduct route over the stretches of water which form the Docklands. Trains run between *05.30-21.50 Mon-Fri. NB: No service Sat & Sun.*

BUSES

Covering the whole of Greater London, the famous red, double-decker buses, with the open platform at the back, are the best way to see London, but they are slower than the tubes, especially in the rush hours (*between 08.00-09.30 & 16.30-18.00 Mon-Fri*). They run from *approx 06.00-24.00 Mon-Sat, 07.30-23.30 Sun.* First and last times of bus routes are indicated on bus stops, but traffic can prevent buses from keeping to them. Buses stop automatically at compulsory bus stops (white background with a red horizontal line through a red circle). At a request stop (red background with a white horizontal line through a white circle) you must raise or wave your arm to hail the bus, and if you want to get off at a request stop, you must ring the bell once, in good time. On driver-only buses, the bells are on the silver hand rails. On open-platform buses, pull the cord overhead downstairs, and push the button at the top of the stairs upstairs. *Fares* are graduated according to zones. The open-platform buses have a conductor who will collect your fare once the bus is moving. The newer buses have only a driver who you must pay as you board the bus. Both give change but do not like being given notes. Keep your ticket until you get off.

Nightbuses run through central London from about *23.00-06.00*. All pass through Trafalgar Square. Consult *Buses for Night Owls* for timetables, available from London Transport and British Rail information centres. Travelcards (except for one-day Travelcards) can be used on nightbuses.

BRITISH RAIL TRAINS

British Rail run InterCity trains all over Britain, and also Network SouthEast, which serves London and the suburbs. Most routes interchange with the underground – timetables are available from the British Travel Centre and other information centres. These trains generally run *06.00-24.00 Mon-Sat, 07.00-22.30 Sun*. *Fares* are graduated and cheap day returns are available except *during the rush hours (08.00-09.30 & 16.30-18.00 Mon-Fri)* and you can also use Travelcards. The Thameslink service gets through London quickly, and goes from Luton Airport via West Hampstead and Blackfriars to Gatwick Airport, Brighton and Kent. Ask at any British Rail station for a timetable.

The main British Rail terminals are:

Blackfriars   **5 C3**
Queen Victoria St EC4. Enquiries: 071-928 5100. Trains to south and south-east London suburbs.

Cannon Street   **5 E3**
Cannon St EC4. Enquiries: 071-928 5100. Trains to south-east London suburbs, Kent and East Sussex.

Charing Cross   **4 F4**
Strand WC2. Enquiries: 071-928 5100. Trains to south-east London suburbs and Kent.

Euston   **1 F4**
Euston Rd NW1. Enquiries: 071-387 7070. Trains to the Midlands, northern England and Scotland.

Fenchurch Street   **5 F3**
Railway Place, Fenchurch St EC3. Enquiries: 071-928 5100. Trains to Essex.

King's Cross   **1 G3**
Euston Rd N1. Enquiries: 071-278 2477. Trains to north-east London suburbs, the Midlands, northern England and Scotland.

Liverpool Street   **5 F1**
Liverpool St EC2. Enquiries: 071-928 5100. Trains to east and north-east London suburbs, Cambridge and East Anglia.

London Bridge   **5 E4**
Borough High St SE1. Enquiries: 071-928 5100. Trains to south-east London suburbs, Kent, Sussex and Surrey.

Marylebone   **1 B5**
Boston Place NW1. Enquiries: 071-262 6767. Trains to west and north-west London suburbs and Buckinghamshire.

Moorgate   **5 E1**
Moorgate EC2. Enquiries: 071-278 2477. Trains to north London suburbs and Hertfordshire.

Paddington   **3 E2**
Praed St W2. Enquiries: 071-262 6767. Trains to west and south-west England and Wales.

St Pancras   **2 A4**
Euston Rd NW1. Enquiries: 071-387 7070. Trains to the Midlands, north-west England and north-west London suburbs.

Victoria   **7 B2**
Terminus Place, Victoria St SW1. Enquiries: 071-928-5100. Trains to south and south-east London suburbs.

Waterloo   **5 B5**
York St SE1. Enquiries: 071-928 5100. Trains to south-west London suburbs, west Surrey, and the south coast of England.

GREEN LINE COACHES

These are express buses run by London Country. Most run from central London to outlying areas within a 40-mile (64km) radius. Main departure point is Eccleston Bridge SW1 (**7 B2**), but there is another departure point on Regent Street just north of Oxford Circus (**4 D2**). For information on schedules and fares phone 081-668 7261.

RIVERBUS

A commuter service linking central London to London City Airport by river. Its route goes via:

Chelsea Harbour
Charing Cross Pier   **4 G4**
Festival Pier (The South Bank Centre)   **4 G4**
Swan Lane Pier (The City)   **5 E3**
London Bridge City Pier   **5 F4**
West India Pier (Docklands & Canary Wharf)
Greenwich Pier
London City Airport Pier
Boats leave *every 20 mins from 07.00-19.40 Mon-Fri (also Sat*

& Sun during summer). Journey from Charing Cross Pier to London City Airport takes *40 mins*. Free timetables available at most piers. For further information phone 071-512 0555.

TAXIS

The famous London black taxi cabs, which can now also be red, blue, green or even white (!) can be hailed in the street. A taxi is available for hire if the yellow 'taxi' sign above the windscreen is lit. If the driver stops, s/he is obliged to take you wherever you want to go, provided the destination is no more than 6 miles (9.6km) – otherwise it is at their discretion. All taxis have meters which the driver must use on all journeys within the Metropolitan Police District (most of Greater London and to Heathrow). For longer journeys the price should be negotiated with the driver beforehand. There is a minimum payable charge which is shown on the meter when you hire a cab. Expect to pay extra for large amounts of luggage, journeys between *20.00-06.00, at weekends and Bank hols*. You can order a black cab by telephone *24hrs* a day, but this will be more expensive than hailing one in the street as you will be charged for being picked up as well as taken to your destination.

Computer-cab: 071-286 0286.
Dial A Cab: 071-253 5000.
Ladycabs: 071-254 3501. Late night cabs for women, driven by women.
Radio Taxicabs: 071-272 0272.

MINICABS

These cannot be hailed in the street, and are indistinguishable from private cars. Unlike black cabs, they are not licensed, nor do their drivers take the same stringent test. The cars have no meters, so it is essential to negotiate the price of each journey in advance. They are usually cheaper than black cabs over long distances, especially *at night and weekends*. Look in the *Yellow Pages* for lists of minicab companies.

Telephone services

ESSENTIAL NUMBERS

999: Emergency (Ambulance, Police, Fire)
100: Operator
155: International operator
142/192: Directory enquiries (142 – London, 192 – national)
153: International directory enquiries
123: Speaking clock
Telegrams: dial 100 and ask for International Telegrams (must be a day in advance).

TO FIND A NUMBER

London residential directories are in two volumes covering the alphabet from A-Z. The business directory covers A-Z in one volume. In addition, *Yellow Pages* also covers all businesses in London listed alphabetically by trade (volumes by region). For directory enquiries (for which there is a charge unless you are calling from a public telephone box) you should have the name and address of the person/company you wish to contact.

MAKING A CALL

London numbers have now been prefixed with 081- and 071- instead of the previous 01-. Generally central London numbers are 071- and Greater London are 081-. If you are not sure which to dial, telephone the operator (100 – free) and they will tell you. It is not necessary to use the prefix when dialling within a zone. The *Code Book* lists all exchanges outside London (or the operator will tell you) including international numbers.

PUBLIC TELEPHONES

The old red telephone boxes have now almost entirely disappeared, to be replaced by glass constructions. They are usually to be found in groups around stations (tube and BR), in hotels, pubs and public places. There are several types:
Coin-operated which take 5p, 10p, 20p, 50p and £1 coins (minimum charge 10p); coins must be inserted before you can dial, but if you do not get through the money will be refunded (it is best to use smaller denominations as percentages of larger ones will not be refunded).
Phonecard which accept only British Telecom phonecards, obtainable at newsagents, chemists, post offices etc and in denominations from 10 units (£1.00) to 200 units (£20.00).
Mercury phonecard which accept only Mercury phonecards (from newsagents, chemists, post offices etc) or credit cards – A.Ax.Dc.V. (minimum charge 50p).

COSTS

These are assessed according to time of day, distance and length of call. There are three different rates: ***Peak***: *09.00-13.00 Mon-Fri*, ***Standard***: *08.00-09.00, 13.00-18.00 Mon-Fri* and ***Cheap***: *18.00-08.00 Mon-Fri & all day and night Sat & Sun*. Cheap time for most international calls is *18.00-08.00*.

Money

CURRENCY

The unit of currency in Britain is the pound sterling (£) divided into 100 pence (p). There are coins for 1p, 2p, 5p, 10p, 20p, 50p and £1, with notes for £5, £10, £20 and £50.

EXCHANGE FACILITIES

There is no exchange control in Britain, so you can carry any amount of money through customs, in or out of the country. The best rate of exchange is always to be found in a bank. Bureaux de change will exchange most currencies and cash cheques, but charge more to do so. They can be found at most airports, main-line stations, central tube stations and in the larger department stores. They operate outside banking hours. Most large hotels will accept travellers' cheques in payment of bills.

Chequepoint Bureau de Change

13 Davies St W1. 071-409 1122.	**4 C3**
220 Earl's Court Rd SW5. 071-373 9515.	**6 A2**
Marble Arch, 548 Oxford St W1. 071-723 2646.	**4 A3**

Eurochange Bureau

95 Buckingham Palace Rd SW1. 071-834 3330.	**7 B2**
Leicester Sq Tube Station WC2. 071-439 2827.	**4 F3**
Paddington Tube Station W2. 071-258 0442.	**3 E2**
Tottenham Court Rd Tube Station W1. 071-734 0279.	**4 E2**

Thomas Cook

123 High Holborn WC1. 071-831 4408.	**4 G1**
104 Kensington High St W8. 071-376 2588.	**3 B6**
100 Victoria St SW1. 071-828 8985.	**7 C1**
Selfridges, 400 Oxford St W1. 071-629 1234.	**4 B2**

BANKS

Standard banking hours are *09.30-15.30 Mon-Fri* although many branches are now open *until 16.30 Mon-Fri and on Sat morning*. They are closed on *Bank holidays* and often close early the *day before a Bank holiday.*

TIPPING

Should be an expression of pleasure for service rendered and never a duty. It is possible not to tip at all if the circumstances justify this. These guidelines give some idea of the average tip:

Restaurants Many add on a service charge, usually 12½%, but do not always say so – if in doubt, ask them. They usually say if it is *not* included.

Taxis 10-15%

Commissionaires for getting a taxi. Up to £1 depending on the effort expended.

Pubs & bars Never at the bar, but buy the barman a drink if you wish. For waiter service in the lounge, from 20p per drink.

Hotels Almost all add it to your bill, usually 10%. Give extra to individuals for special service, from 50p.

Porters 50p-£1 per case depending on how far it is carried.

Car hire

*The law now states that **all** occupants of the car must wear safety belts. This includes the driver, and all passengers, (although it only applies to back seat passengers if safety belts have already been fitted). **Don't** park on double yellow lines, it will result in a parking fine or wheelclamp (both are expensive).*
To hire a car you will normally need to be over 21 and to have held a licence, valid for use in the UK, for at least a year. Overseas visitors' licences are valid in Britain for a year. Prices differ greatly from company to company and depending on the make of car and the season. There is a basic daily, weekly or monthly charge and you will be required to leave a deposit.

Avis   **4 B5**
10 Montrose Place SW1. 071-245 9862. You can book a car for anywhere in London from here. *Open 07.30-19.30 Mon-Sun.* World-wide reservations: 081-848 8733.

Eurodollar
Warwick Place, Uxbridge, Middx. (0895) 233300. Book for London or worldwide from this office. *Open 08.00-18.00 Mon-Fri, 08.30-16.00 Sat.*

Hertz
Radnor House, 1272 London Rd SW16. 081-679 1799. Branches throughout London, Great Britain and the Continent. *Open 08.00-18.00 Mon-Fri, to 17.00 Sat.*

Bicycle hire

The bike offers an alternative and often more interesting form of transport. London has become far more geared to cyclists in recent years and there are now special cycle lanes on many roads. Danger to health from noxious fumes is not nearly as great as the benefit gained from the exercise of cycling. Explore streets, relax in parks and avoid parking difficulties!

London Bicycle Tours   **5 B4**
56 Upper Ground SE1. 071-928 6838. Also organises tours. *Open May-Sep 11.00-18.00 Mon-Sun; Oct-Apr by appointment.*

On Your Bike   **5 E4**
22 Duke Street Hill SE1. 071-357 6958. *Open 09.00-18.00, 09.30-16.30 Sat.*

Portobello Cycles
69 Golborne Rd W10. 081-960 0444. *Open 10.00-17.00 Mon-Sat.*

HISTORIC LONDON

London's history begins in AD43, when invading Romans bridged the Thames. They built the London Wall around AD200, traces of which are still visible today. This was to determine the shape of what is still called the City of London for some 1300 years. Despite the devastation of three-fifths of the City during the Great Fire of 1666, no radical replanning took place immediately within the 'Square Mile'. However, a massive scheme grew out of the ashes beyond the City, which was to create the London we know today. Surrounding villages were absorbed and now give their names to central districts of the capital.

London's growth resulted from rising commercial importance (the City is still one of the world's major financial centres), the Industrial Revolution, and more recently developing public transport which pushed new suburbs well out into the countryside.

London has, naturally, changed enormously through the years, but, despite the Blitz and decades of redevelopment, every stage of London's history can be traced through her buildings, monuments, churches and famous houses.

Historic sights and buildings

Admiralty Arch   4 E4
Entrance to the Mall SW1. Massive Edwardian triple arch by Sir Aston Webb 1911. A memorial to Queen Victoria.

Albert Memorial   3 E5
Kensington Gore SW7. Gothic memorial to Queen Victoria's consort, Prince Albert, by Sir George Gilbert Scott, 1872. It is 175ft (53.3m) high with a 14ft (4.3m) statue of the Prince by John Foley.

Apsley House   4 B5
149 Piccadilly W1. 071-499 5676. Originally known as 'Number One London', home of the 1st Duke of Wellington. Robert Adam 1778, alterations by Wyatt 1828. Now a museum. *Closed for restoration at time of publication.*

BBC Broadcasting House   1 D6
Portland Place W1. 071-743 8000. G.Val Myers 1928. Imposing headquarters of the British Broadcasting Corporation where the Director-General and Governors meet to discuss the BBCs broadcasting policy.

Bank of England 5 E2

Threadneedle St EC2. 071-601 4444. The government and bankers' bank and custodian of the nation's gold reserves. Outer walls are the original design of Sir John Soane, architect to the Bank 1788-1833. Interior redesigned by Sir Herbert Baker 1925-39. Bank of England Museum (see p53) *open to the public.*

Banqueting House 4 F4

Whitehall SW1. 071-930 4179. Inigo Jones 1619-25. Only surviving part of Whitehall Palace, used for state and court ceremonies. *Open 10.00-17.00 Tue-Sat, 14.00-17.00 Sun. Closed Mon except Bank hols.* Charge.

Barbican 5 C1

Silk St EC2. Chamberlin, Powell and Bon 1955. Over 2000 apartments (some the highest in Europe when built), a water garden, the restored St Giles Cripplegate Church, a girls' school, pubs, shops, a museum and the Barbican Centre (1982) – the largest arts centre in the country.

British Telecom Tower 1 E6

Howland St W1. Eric Bedford 1966. Stands 580ft (176.7m) high topped by a 39ft (11.9m) mast with radar aerial. Houses telecommunications equipment and offices.

Buckingham Palace 4 D5

St James's Park SW1. 071-930 4832. The official London residence of the Queen. Built 1705, enlarged by Nash 1825. 600 rooms, 12 occupied by Queen Elizabeth II and the Duke of Edinburgh. The Royal Standard is flown when the Queen is in residence.

Burlington Arcade 4 D3

Piccadilly W1. 1819 Regency arcade famous for small, exclusive shops. Beadles still ensure obedience to rules forbidding 'singing, carrying large parcels, and running'!

Canary Wharf Tower

West India Docks, Isle of Dogs E14. Tallest building in the United Kingdom, 800ft (244m) high, set in an 80-acre (35ha) 'new district' with shops, offices, apartments, restaurants and waterfront promenades.

Carnaby Street 4 D3

W1. The first men's boutique opened in 1957. World famous by the 1960s and the heart of fashion during the following swinging decade, especially for pop stars. Still has a lively, if not so fashionable, image.

The Cenotaph 4 F5

Whitehall SW1. Sir Edwin Lutyens (1920) to honour the dead of the First World War, and now those who died in both World Wars. The word comes from the Greek *kenos* meaning empty and *taphos* meaning tomb. The annual Service of Remembrance takes place here in *November* (see p52).

Chelsea Royal Hospital   7 A3
Royal Hospital Rd SW3. 071-730 0161. Established 1682 by
Charles II for veteran soldiers. Designed by Wren and opened
in 1689 admitting 476 army pensioners. Fine carvings, several
royal portraits and a museum. *Open 10.00-12.00 & 14.00-
16.00 Mon-Sat, 14.00-16.00 Sun.* Free.

Clarence House   4 D5
Stable Yard Gate SW1. Elegant stuccoed mansion by Nash
1825. Now the home of the Queen Mother.

Cleopatra's Needle   5 A3
Victoria Embankment SW1. Brought from Heliopolis, dates to
1500 BC. Presented by Egypt and erected here 1878.

Covent Garden   4 F3
WC2. Originally designed by Inigo Jones as a residential
square in the 1630s. Market buildings by Fowler 1830; Floral
Hall added 1860 by E.M. Barry, architect of the Royal Opera
House (1858). In 1974 the flower market moved to Nine Elms
(**7 D5**), but the area survived to become a flourishing new
community, with an eclectic, though expensive range of
shops, and places to eat and drink.

Docklands
The once prosperous London docks fell into decline in the
1960s as sea traffic moved downstream to Tilbury. New
development began in the the mid-1980s and continues
unabated. Neglected wharves have been given a new lease of
life, with St Katharine's Dock (**5 G3**) the first to be converted
into shops, restaurants and a hotel. Other areas worth exploring
are Tobacco Dock, and West India Dock on the Isle of Dogs.

Downing Street   4 F5
SW1. Built by Sir George Downing MP in 17thC. No.10 is the
official residence of the Prime Minister; No.11 that of the
Chancellor of the Exchequer, and No.12 is the Party Whips'
Office. *Wrought-iron gates prevent direct public access.*

Fleet Street   5 B2
EC4. London's 'Street of Ink', associated with printing since
Caxton, has now lost most of its newspapers as new technology
moved them elsewhere. Connections still remain.

Greenwich
Cutty Sark
King William Walk SE10. 081-858 3445. One of the great tea
clippers, built 1869, now in dry dock. Explore the galley and
cabins. Next to it is *Gipsy Moth IV*, in which Sir Francis
Chichester sailed single-handed round the world in 1966. Both
*open Apr-Sep 10.00-17.30 Mon-Sat, 12.00-17.30 Sun; Oct-Mar
10.00-16.30 Mon-Sat, 12.00-16.30 Sun.* Charge.

Museum of Artillery
The Rotunda, Repository Rd, Woolwich Common SE18. 081-

854 2242 x 3128. Pavilion by Nash, 1822. A renowned collection of guns and muskets, rifles, armour and early rockets from France, Burma, Britain and India. *Open 12.30-16.30 Mon-Fri, 14.00-16.00 Sat & Sun*. Voluntary donation.

Old Royal Observatory
Greenwich Park SE10. 081-858 1167. Part of the National Maritime Museum and including Flamsteed House. Founded by Charles II in 1675 and designed by Wren. Stand astride the Meridien line to be in both the eastern and western hemispheres at the same time. Extensive collection of time-measuring instruments. *Open Apr-Sep 10.00-18.00 Mon-Sat, 14.00-18.00 Sun; Oct-Mar 10.00-17.00 Mon-Fri, 10.00-17.30 Sat, 14.00-17.00 Sun*. Charge.

Royal Naval College
Greenwich SE10. 081-858 2154. On the site of Greenwich Palace, Wren's beautiful baroque building, 1694, houses Sir James Thornhill's amazing Painted Hall (which took 20 years to complete). *Open 14.30-17.00 Mon-Wed & Fri-Sun*. Free.

Guildhall   5 D2
Off Gresham St EC2. 071-606 3030. Built 1411-40 with alterations by George Dance 1789 and Sir Giles Gilbert Scott 1953. Great Hall used for ceremonial occasions – there was a banquet here to celebrate Queen Elizabeth II's coronation. Library established 1423. Medieval crypt the most extensive of its kind in London. Great Hall *open 09.00-17.30 Mon-Sat*. Free. Library *open 09.30-17.00 Mon-Sat*. Free.

Hampton Court Palace
Hampton Court, Middx. 081-977 8441. Riverside Tudor palace built 1514 for Cardinal Wolsey and acquired (in a rather one-sided bargain!) by Henry VIII who greatly enlarged it. Later additions by Wren in the 1690s for William III and Mary. Sumptuous state rooms decorated by Vanbrugh, Verrio and Thornhill. Famous picture gallery of Italian masterpieces, the Orangery, the Great Vine and the Maze. Spectacular formal gardens. *Open Apr-Sep 09.30-18.00 Mon-Sat, 11.00-18.00 Sun; Oct-Mar 09.30-17.00 Mon-Sat, 14.00-17.00 Sun*. Charge.

Houses of Parliament   4 F6
St Margaret St SW1. 071-219 3000. Originally the Palace of Westminster and a principal royal palace until 1512. Became known as 'parliament' or 'place to speak' in 1550. Westminster Hall, one of the few remaining parts of the original palace, has an impressive hammerbeam roof. The present Victorian Gothic building was designed in 1847 by Sir Charles Barry and Augustus Pugin specifically to house Parliament and has over 1100 rooms, 100 staircases and over 2 miles (3.2 km) of passages. Recently cleaned to reveal their full architectural beauty, the Houses of Parliament and Big Ben – the bell clock

housed in the adjoining St Stephen's Tower – make up London's most famous landmark. *To arrange a visit or tour contact your local MP for advance tickets to the Visitor's Gallery or queue at St Stephen's entrance (there are very long queues in summer advisable to go after 17.00 to avoid them). No small children allowed.* Free.

Hyde Park Corner   **4 B5**
SW1. Constitution Arch and the Ionic Screen of three classical-style triumphal arches by Decimus Burton 1825. Once intended as an imposing and pleasing feature of the journey from Buckingham Palace to Hyde Park, it now swarms with traffic and underground pedestrians.

Inns of Court
There are four great Inns of Court, dating from the 14thC, which act as a law school and have the exclusive privilege of calling candidates to the English Bar. Before they are eligible to be called, prospective barristers must pass the Bar exams, join one of the four Inns of Court and dine 24 times in the halls.

Gray's Inn   **5 B1**
Holborn WC1 (entrance from passage next to 22 High Holborn). 071-405 8164. An Inn of Court since the 14thC, although the oldest surviving buildings are 17thC. Francis Bacon had chambers here from 1577 until his death. He reportedly laid out the gardens and planted the Catalpa trees. *Open 10.00-16.00 Mon-Fri.* Free.

Lincoln's Inn   **5 A2**
WC2. 071-405 1393. Parts of Lincoln's Inn date back to the 13thC, and it still has a Dickensian atmosphere. Famous members include Disraeli, Gladstone and Oliver Cromwell. *Open 10.00-16.00 Mon-Fri (gardens open 12.30-14.30 only). Closed Sat & Sun. Admission to the chapel outside these hours and to the Hall and Library by application to the Treasury Office, Whitehall SW1.* Free.

Inner Temple   **5 B2**
Crown Office Row EC4. 071-353 8462. The Inner Temple dates from 1505. Prince Henry's Room, above the Gateway (1610), is the oldest domestic building in London and home to the Samuel Pepys Club and Pepysian memorabilia. *Open 10.00-16.00 Mon-Fri by arrangement. Closed Sat, Sun, Bank hols & legal vacations.*

Middle Temple   **5 B3**
Middle Temple Lane EC4. 071-353 4355. Dates from 1570. Together with the Inner Temple it comprises courtyards, alleys, gardens and warm brick buildings. *Open 10.00-11.30 & 15.00-16.00 Mon-Fri by arrangement. Closed Sat, Sun, Bank hols, Aug & during examinations.* Free.

Jewel Tower   **4 F6**

Old Palace Yard SW1. 071-222 2219. 14thC surviving frag-
ment of the Palace of Westminster, once the safe for Edward
III's jewels, clothes and furs, now home to a collection of
objects found during excavations of the area. *Open Easter-Sep
10.00-13.00 & 14.00-18.00 Mon-Sun; Oct-Easter 10.00-13.00
& 14.00-16.00 Mon-Sun.* Free.

Kensington Palace   **3 C4**

Kensington Gardens W8. 071-937 9561. Unostentatious house
by Wren bought 1689 by William III. Orangery House by
Hawksmoor and Vanbrugh for Queen Anne in 1704. Queen
Victoria was born here. Princess Margaret and the Prince and
Princess of Wales have apartments here. State apartments
*open 09.00-17.00 Mon-Sat, 13.00-17.00 Sun (last admission
16.15).* Charge.

Kenwood House (Iveagh Bequest)

Hampstead Lane NW3. 071-348 1286. Robert Adam 1764-9.
Edward Guinness, 1st Earl of Iveagh's collection of paintings
including works by van Dyck, Reynolds, Rembrandt,
Gainsborough and Turner. Gardens and wooded estate of 200
acres (81ha). *Open Easter-Sep 10.00-18.00 Mon-Sun; Oct-
Easter 10.00-16.00 Mon-Sun.* Free.

Lambeth Palace   **7 F1**

Lambeth Palace Rd SE1. 071-928 8282. Official London
residence of the Archbishop of Canterbury since 1197. 13thC
crypt beneath the chapel and Tudor gatehouse. The gloves
worn by Charles I when he went to the scaffold are displayed
along with a brass plate commemorating the negligence of the
gardener who stuck his fork through Archbishop Laud's
tortoise. *Tours (very restricted) Wed or Thur by written
application to the Booking Secretary.* Charge.

Law Courts   **5 B2**

Strand WC2. 071-936 6000. Massive Victorian-Gothic building
housing the Royal Courts of Justice. More than 1000 rooms
and 3½ miles of corridor. *Open to public 09.00-16.30 Mon-Fri.*
Over 16s only. Courts not in session *Aug & Sep but still open
to the public.* Free.

Lloyds of London   **5 F2**

Lime St EC3. 071-623 7100. Impressive glass and aluminium
structure, by the Richard Rogers Partnership (jointly responsible
for the Pompidou Centre in Paris). Spectacular at night, this
multi-faceted, 12-storey structure is the headquarters for the
international insurance market. Huge dealing room in a 246ft-
(75m) high atrium housing the famous Lutine Bell.

London Wall   **5 D1**

EC2. Parts of the old Roman wall still survives at St Alphage
Garden, St Giles Churchyard, Cripplegate St EC1 (**5 D1**); Jewry

St EC3 (**5 G2**); off Trinity Square EC3 (**5 F3**) and in the Tower of London (**5 G3**).

Mansion House   5 E2
Walbrook EC4. 071-626 2500. Official residence of the Lord Mayor of London, built 1739 by George Dance the Elder. Palladian mansion with several majestic rooms such as the Ball Room, Banqueting Room, and Egyptian Hall, lavishly decorated in 23-carat gold. *Closed for renovation at time of publication.*

Marble Arch   3 G3
W1. John Nash 1827, based on the Arch of Constantine in Rome. Only senior members of the Royal Family and the King's Troop Royal Horse Artillery may pass through it.

Monument   5 E3
Monument St EC3. 071-626 2717. Wren 1671-7. Made of Portland stone, it commemorates the Great Fire of 1666 and stands at 202ft (61.5m), a foot in height for every foot in distance from where the fire started in Pudding Lane. Summit 311 steps up spiral staircase. Magnificent views. *Open Apr-Sep 09.00-17.40 Mon-Fri, 14.00-17.40 Sat & Sun; Oct-Mar 09.00-15.40 Mon-Sat.* Charge.

NatWest Tower   5 F2
Bishopsgate EC2. 1980. 600ft (183m) tower – tallest building in Britain until the Canary Wharf Tower was completed in 1990 (see p29). Slender, shining structure with a curious pin-striped effect from the closeness of its vertical lines. Dominates City skyline and houses the head offices of the National Westminster Bank.

Nelson's Column   4 E4
Trafalgar Sq WC2. By William Railton 1839-42, 145ft (44m) column surmounted by a 16ft (5m) stone statue of Admiral Lord Nelson by E.H. Baily, erected 1843. The statue is minus his eye and arm, both lost in battle.

Old Bailey   5 C2
Old Bailey EC4. 071-248 3277. Central Criminal Court, on the site of the old Newgate Prison. The scene for many famous trials – Oscar Wilde in 1895, Dr Crippen in 1910, J.R. Christie in 1953 and Peter Sutcliffe, 'the Yorkshire Ripper', in 1981. Public viewing gallery. *Open 10.30-13.00 & 14.00-16.00 Mon-Fri. Minimum age 14 (must be accompanied by an adult if under 16).* Free.

Pall Mall   4 D4
SW1. Early 19thC opulence. Gentlemen's clubs were established on this fine street as exclusive havens for their members. Reform Club, (No.104) by Charles Barry, from where the fictitious character Phileas Fogg began his trip *Around the World in 80 Days*; Travellers' Club (No.106) founded

1819; Athenaeum Club (No.107), founded for the intellectually elite.

Piccadilly Circus   **4 E3**

W1. The confluence of five major thoroughfares – Regent Street, Shaftesbury Avenue, Haymarket, Piccadilly and Lower Regent Street. Fountain and statue of Eros by Gilbert (1893). The world-famous neon advertising hoardings make it a far cry from its original elegant designs. The first, for Bovril and Schweppes at the turn of the century, caused a great scandal. The London Pavilion and Trocadero Centre present one-stop shopping and modern requirements.

Regent Street   **4 D3**

John Nash, asked by George IV (then Prince of Wales) to construct a link from Carlton House (now demolished) to the royal country home near Regent's Park, not only designed the route for Regent Street but also most of the buildings along it. This took many years since it was pieced together to conform with various architectural styles along the way. Initially acclaimed, its imminent destruction was celebrated in 1927 when George V and his Queen drove down its flower-decked length – it was then rebuilt from end to end.

Ritz Hotel   **4 D4**

Piccadilly W1. 071-493 8181. Designed by César Ritz 1906. Archways based on the rue de Rivoli in Paris, interior in Louis XVI style.

Royal Albert Hall   **3 E5**

Kensington Gore SW7. 071-589 8212. Originally built as the 'Hall of Arts & Sciences', prefixed with 'Royal Albert' at the last minute by Queen Victoria. Oval, not circular, as you might imagine, this is the venue for a wide variety of events from organ recitals to boxing matches. *Guided tours Jun-mid Sep 10.00, 12.00, 14.00 & 15.30 Mon-Sun.* Charge.

Royal Exchange   **5 E2**

cnr Threadneedle St & Cornhill EC3. Present building (the third) 1844 by Sir William Tite. Original destroyed in the Great Fire. Since 1982 home to the London International Financial Futures Exchange (LIFFE). More than 20,000 contracts are exchanged per day here. Watch the dealers in action. *Open to the public 11.30-14.00 Mon-Fri.* Free.

St James's Palace   **4 D4**

Pall Mall SW1. Built by Henry VIII for Anne Boleyn and used as a royal palace for over 300 years. Still a royal residence although no members of the royal family live there at present. Foreign ambassadors and High Commissioners are still accredited to the Court of St James although actually received at Buckingham Palace. Courtyards only *open to the public.*

Savile Row   **4 D3**
W1. World-famous as the headquarters of the finest of
London's tailors. Built 1730s as a residential street, it became
fashionable amongst tailors from the mid-19thC.

Savoy Hotel   **4 G3**
Strand WC2. Richard D'Oyly Carte 1889. Impeccable and
impressive standards. Monet painted Waterloo Bridge from its
terraces. Still the favourite of the famous.

Soho   **4 D2**
An area bounded by Regent Street, Oxford Street,
Shaftesbury Avenue and Charing Cross Road. Lively and
notorious but perfectly safe, except for a handful of peep
shows and strip joints. Narrow 18th and 19thC streets full of
fascinating foreign food shops, restaurants, street markets,
flashing neon and nightlife of all sorts. Chinatown radiates
from Gerrard Street.

Somerset House   **4 G3**
Strand WC2. On the site of an unfinished Renaissance palace
(1547-50) with a history of many royal inhabitants. Present
building by Sir William Chambers 1776. Once housed the register of births, marriages and deaths in England and Wales
(see Public Record Office on p58), now holds the register of
divorce, wills and probate, offices of the Inland Revenue and
the Courtauld Institute Galleries (see p54). *Open 10.00-16.00
Mon-Fri.* Free.

Spitalfields   **5 G1**
E1. This centre of silk-weaving in England was established by
the influx of Flemish and French weavers in the 16thC and
17thC. The industry reached its height at the end of the 18thC
and early 19thC when about 17,000 looms were in use and a
large area of East London was dependent on these family con-
cerns. Fournier Street has some good examples of Dutch-style
houses of the time. The industry collapsed some 100 years ago,
but the streets here are still steeped in history and tradition.

Thames Barrier
Unity Way, Eastmoor St SE18. 081-854 1373. Steel fins form
an impressive piece of modern engineering set up to stem
dangerously high tides. Completed in 1982, it is the world's
largest moveable flood barrier. The Visitor Centre houses an
exhibition explaining the technology involved. *25-min* cruise
from Barrier Pier. *Open 10.30-17.00 Mon-Sun.* Charge.

Tower of London   **5 G3**
Tower Hill EC3. 071-709 0765. A keep, a prison and still a
fortress, the Tower has served as a palace, place of execution
and in its time has housed the Royal Mint, the Royal
Observatory, the Royal Menagerie, and the Public Records.
Now famous for the Bloody Tower, Traitors' Gate, the ravens,

the Crown Jewels, the Armouries and the Yeomen Warders (or Beefeaters). British monarchs imprisoned here include Edward III, Henry VII and Elizabeth I. Other prisoners have included Thomas More; Guy Fawkes and his fellow plotters; Sir Walter Ralegh; and Rudolf Hess, detained during World War II. Also the site of many executions including two of Henry VIII's wives – Anne Boleyn in 1536, and Catherine Howard in 1542, both of whom were given the privilege of a quiet execution on Tower Green. The Yeomen Warders still guard the Crown Jewels, with which the new monarch is invested at the coronation ceremony. *Open Mar-Oct 09.30-17.45 Mon-Sat, 14.00-17.45 Sun; Nov-Feb 09.30-16.00 Mon-Sat. Be prepared for long queues in summer.* Charge.

Trafalgar Square   **4 F4**
WC2. Laid out by Sir Charles Barry 1829. Nelson's column (see p34) stands in the middle surrounded by Landseers four impressive bronze lions, 1868. Fountains by Lutyens. Famous for political rallies, pigeons and the excesses of New Year's Eve revellers.

Whitehall   **4 F4**
Wide thoroughfare once part of the ancient main route linking Westminster and the City, now used for ceremonial and State processions. Lined with Government offices including Old Admiralty, Old Scotland Yard, the War Office, the Foreign Office, Dover House, the Treasury, Horse Guards' Parade and Banqueting House.

Whittington Stone
Highgate Hill N6. Near the junction with Dartmouth Park Hill. The milestone marks the spot where tradition says Dick Whittington, London's most famous Lord Mayor, heard the Bow Bells chime 'Turn again, Whittington, thrice Lord Mayor of London'.

Houses of the famous

Carlyle's house   **6 E4**
24 Cheyne Row SW3. 071-352 7087. Modest Queen Anne terrace where Carlyle lived for 42 years until his death in 1881. Ruskin, Dickens and Kingsley were frequent visitors. *Open 11.00-17.00 (last admission 16.30) Wed-Sun & Bank hols except Good Fri. Closed Nov-Mar.* Charge.

Dickens' house   **2 B5**
48 Doughty St WC1. 071-405 2127. Regency terraced house where Charles Dickens and his family lived from 1837-9. Here he completed *The Pickwick Papers* and wrote *Oliver Twist* and *Nicholas Nickleby. Open 10.00-17.00 (last admission 16.30). Closed Sun & Bank hols.* Charge.

Freud Museum
20 Maresfield Gdns, Hampstead NW3. 071-435 2002. Exactly as it was when he died in 1939, the house in which Sigmund Freud found refuge after fleeing Hitler in 1938. Extraordinary collection of Egyptian, Greek, Roman and Oriental antiquities and Freud's personal effects. Also the famous couch on which he conducted his analyses. *Open 12.00-17.00 Wed-Sun.* Charge.

Hogarth's house
Hogarth Lane, Great West Rd, Chiswick W4. 081-994 6757. William Hogarth's home from 1749 until his death in 1764. Relics and impressions of his engravings on display. *Open Apr-Sep 11.00-18.00 Mon & Wed-Sat, 14.00-18.00 Sun; Oct-Mar 11.00-16.00 Mon & Wed-Sat, 14.00-16.00 Sun. Closed Tue, first two weeks of Sep & last three weeks of Dec.* Free.

Dr Johnson's house   5 B2
17 Gough St, Fleet St EC4. 071-353 3745. 17thC house in the attic of which Dr Samuel Johnson compiled his famous dictionary. Lived here from 1748-59. Relics include his chair from the Old Cock Tavern and a first edition of his dictionary. *Open May-Sep 11.00-17.30 Mon-Sat; Oct-Apr 11.00-17.00 Mon-Sat. Closed Sun & Bank hols.* Small charge.

Keats' House
Wentworth Place, Keats Grove, Hampstead NW3. 071-435 2062. The poet John Keats lived here from 1818-20, during which time his love affair with Fanny Brawne began. *Ode to a Nightingale* was composed in the garden in a single morning. *Open Apr-Oct 14.00-18.00 Mon-Fri, 10.00-13.00 & 14.00-17.00 Sat, 14.00-17.00 Sun & Bank hols; Nov-Mar 13.00-17.00 Mon-Fri, 10.00-13.00 & 14.00-17.00 Sat, 14.00-17.00 Sun & Bank hols.* Free.

Leighton House   3 A6
12 Holland Park Rd W14. 071-602 3316. Eastern-style house, commissioned by Lord Frederick Leighton 1866. Arab Hall decorated with 14th-16thC oriental tiles. Paintings by Leighton and Burne-Jones. Watts and De Morgan pottery. *Open 11.00-17.00 Mon-Sat. Closed Sun & Bank hols.* Free.

Wesley's house & chapel   2 D3
47 City Rd EC1. 071-253 2262. Methodist John Wesley's possessions and personal relics, and his tomb in the nearby chapel. In the crypt a museum tells the story of Methodism. *Open 10.00-16.00 Mon-Sat, 12.00-15.00 Sun.* Small charge.

Places of worship

In their buildings, ruins, sites and associations, London's churches and cathedrals represent nearly 1400 years of Christianity in Britain. The Great Fire of 1666 set the scene for Wren's rebuilding programme, including St Paul's Cathedral and 50 other churches. The 17thC and early 18thC saw many more churches built, to the designs of Nicholas Hawksmoor and Inigo Jones, and the Victorians produced a wealth of new churches in the 19thC.

Non-Christian religions also have their part in London's history, with synagogues as at Bevis Marks and, most recently, the London Central Mosque in Regent's Park for London's growing Islamic community.

Entrance to all places of worship is free, unless otherwise stated.

All Souls, Langham Place   **4 C1**
Langham Place W1. 071-580 4357. Nash's only church, 1822-24. Unusual style – Corinthian columns and needle spire. Interior refitted 1976. Exterior restored 1987-8.

Bevis Marks Synagogue   **5 F2**
Heneage Lane (off Bevis Marks) EC3. 071-626 1274. Built in 1700, Britain's oldest surviving synagogue. Fine windows and brass chandeliers from Amsterdam.

Brompton Oratory   **3 F6**
Brompton Rd SW3. 071-589 4811. Baroque style, Herbert Gribble 1834. The centre of Roman Catholicism until Westminster Cathedral was built 1903. Ornate interior and fine statues, some originals from Cathedral of Siena.

Chapel Royal of St John   **5 G3**
White Tower, Tower of London EC3. 071-709 0765. The oldest Norman church in London, c1085. Original pillars still intact.

Chelsea Old Church, All Saints   **6 E4**
Chelsea Embankment SW3. 071-352 5627. Henry VIII and Jane Seymour married here in 1536. Original church dates from 1157, but the south chapel was rebuilt by Sir Thomas More. Severely bombed in 1941 and restored by Walter Godfrey. Many historic monuments.

London Central Mosque   **1 A4**
Hanover Gate, Regent's Park NW1. 071-724 3363. Graceful building completed 1978, the religious centre for London's Muslims. A 75ft (25m)-high golden dome and rich interior – marble floors, Turkish tiles, Iranian carpets and Jordanian chandeliers.

St Bartholomew-the-Great   **5 C1**
West Smithfield EC1. 071-606 1575. Oldest church in London – the only surviving part of an Augustinian priory founded in 1123. Unusual oriel window and the only pre-Reformation font in the City. Many fine monuments.

St Clement Danes   **4 F3**
Strand WC2. 071-242 8282. First built by Danes in 9thC, rebuilt by Wren 1681. Destroyed during the Blitz, restored and rededicated in 1958 as the central church of the RAF. Bells

ring 'Oranges and Lemons', made famous by the nursery
rhyme of the same name.

St Giles Cripplegate   **5 D1**
Fore St EC2. 071-606 3630. 12thC church rebuilt 1537 and
restored by Godfrey Allen 1952 after bombing. Milton is buried
here. Remains of the London Wall in churchyard.

St James Piccadilly   **4 D3**
Piccadilly W1. 071-734 4511. Wren 1684. Restored by Sir
Albert Richardson 1954 after serious bomb damage. Reredos,
organ casing and font by Grinling Gibbons. Famous 'Father
Smith' organ presented by Queen Mary 1691 and brought
from Whitehall Palace.

St John Smith Square   **4 F6**
Smith Sq SW1. 071-222 2168. Nicknamed 'Queen Anne's
Footstool'. Built 1721-8 by Archer, gutted by fire 1742. Interior
redesigned, then blitzed 1941. Restored to original design by a
charitable trust. Opened as concert hall 1969.

St Margaret Westminster   **4 F5**
Parliament Sq SW1. 071-222 6382. Rebuilt 1486-1523 and
after World War II. Splendid early 16thC east window and
stained glass by Piper. Parish church of House of Commons
since 1614. Samuel Pepys married here 1655, John Milton in
1656 and Winston Churchill in 1908. Caxton, Walter Ralegh
and Admiral Blake are buried here.

St Martin-in-the-Fields   **4 F4**
Trafalgar Sq WC2. 071-930 1862. Founded 12thC, rebuilt
many times. Present construction by Gibbs 1722-4 with
famous spire and portico. In 1924 the first broadcast service
was conducted from here. Charles II christened here 1630;
Nell Gwynne, Hogarth, Sir Joshua Reynolds buried here. Brass
rubbing centre, craft market, restaurant and gallery.

St Mary-le-Bow   **5 D2**
Cheapside EC2. 071-248 5139. Famous for its bells, used
before World War II as time signal by BBC. True Cockneys are
born within hearing distance of them. Rebuilt Wren 1670-83
and again by King 1956-62. Superb steeple – 217ft (66m).

St Paul's Cathedral   **5 D2**
Ludgate Hill EC4. 071-248 4619/2705. Wren's masterpiece is
the fifth cathedral on this site. The Whispering Gallery in the
dome is particularly impressive – so named because the
quietest whisper carries from one side to the other – 107ft
(33m) away. Choir stalls and organ by Grinling Gibbons.
Nelson and the Duke of Wellington are buried here; the Prince
and Princess of Wales were married here in 1981. *Open
08.00-18.00 Mon-Sun except during special services.* Free.
Crypt, ambulatory and galleries *open 10.00-16.15 Mon-Fri,
11.00-16.15 Sat.* Charge.

St Peter-upon-Cornhill 5 E2

Cornhill EC3. 071-626 9483. Very fine church by Wren, 1677-87. Oldest church site in the City, reputedly AD179. Organ built by Schmidt. Fine carved screen.

Southwark Cathedral 5 E4

Borough High St SE1. 071-407 2939. Originally founded in the 7thC, this is one of London's earliest Gothic churches. The tower dates to 1520 and the collection of monuments includes an oak effigy of a knight, dating to around 1275. The Chapter House has been redeveloped and now includes a restaurant. Cathedral *open 08.00-18.00 Mon-Sun.* Chapter House Restaurant *open 10.00-16.00 Mon-Fri.*

Temple Church 5 B2

Inner Temple, Crown Office Row EC4. 071-353 8462. One of only four remaining early Gothic round churches built by the Knight Templars, 12thC-13thC.

Westminster Abbey 4 F6

Broad Sanctuary SW1. 071-222 5152. Original church founded by Edward the Confessor 1065. Rebuilding commenced 1245 by Henry III and largely completed by 1506. Towers completed by Hawksmoor 1734. Since William I it has been the coronation church of every new monarch and houses the coronation chair. Many royal and historic figures buried here, along with the Unknown Warrior, whose tomb represents the dead of World War I. Poets' Corner is the resting place of Dryden, Browning, Sheridan and Tennyson. Sculpted angels in south transept and fine tiled floors. *Open 08.00-18.00 Mon-Sun.* Royal Chapels *open 09.00-14.45 & 16.00-16.45 Sat* (charge), *18.00-19.45 Wed* (free). *Closed Sun, services only.* Museum *open 10.30-16.00 Mon-Sat.* Small charge.

Westminster RC Cathedral 4 D6

Ashley Place SW1. 071-834 7452. The headquarters of the Catholic Church in Britain. Completed 1903, with glorious marble mosaics. Widest nave in England with the early 15thC statue of Our Lady and Child. *Open 07.00-20.00 Mon-Sun.*

London's bridges

Albert Bridge 6 E4

Three-span bridge 1871 by Ordish. Unusual rigid chain suspension. Tradition has it that soldiers crossing must break step because their marching rhythm may weaken the structure! Particularly beautiful at night when illuminated.

Chelsea Bridge 7 B4

Original bridge built 1858 by Page. Human bones and Roman and British weapons tell of an immense battle fought here. Entirely replaced in 1934 by a suspension bridge.

Lambeth Bridge   7 E2
The site of the first bridge at Lambeth was originally the only place where a coach and horses could cross the river. In 1633 Archbishop Laud sank the coach with his belongings whilst moving into Lambeth Palace! First bridge constructed 1861, replaced 1929.

London Bridge   5 E4
Reigned supreme as the only bridge for 500 years. Originally wooden construction built by Romans, replaced in 12thC with stone one carrying houses, shops and the heads of traitors on spikes. Replaced many times – in 1971 the granite construction by Rennie (1832) was shipped off in its entirety to Lake Havasu City, Arizona. Present bridge 1973.

Queen Elizabeth II Bridge
London's newest bridge, opened October 1991. The first bridge downstream since Tower Bridge built 1894. Designed to ease the weight of traffic through Dartford Tunnel. Largest of its type in Europe – twin towers 450ft (130m) high. Toll charges will be incurred until around the year 2005.

Tower Bridge   5 G4
Jones and Wolfe-Barry 1894. Designed to echo the Tower of London. It opens to allow tall ships to pass – each section of the double-bascule drawbridge weighs over 1000 tonnes but can be raised in under two minutes. High walkways afford excellent views of London and the Thames. Museum displays illustrate the workings of the bridge (*open Apr-Oct 10.00-18.30 Mon-Sun; Nov-Mar 10.00-16.45 Mon-Sun.* Charge).

Waterloo Bridge   4 G3
Rennie 1811. Opened on the anniversary of the Battle of Waterloo. Present bridge by Sir Giles Gilbert Scott 1937-42.

Westminster Bridge   4 F5
The watermen of the Thames were paid £25,000 in compensation when the bridge was begun in 1738. A stern warning went out when it opened – no dogs and the death penalty for anyone found defacing its walls! Present structure graceful cast iron, 1854 by Page.

Statues and monuments

Achilles   4 B4
Park Lane W1. 20ft (6.5m) bronze by Westmacott 1822. Caused an uproar as it was a nude statue dedicated by the 'women of England' to the Duke of Wellington.

Alfred the Great   5 D6
Trinity Church Sq SE1. Unknown origins, but undoubtedly the oldest statue in London, dating to the 14thC.

Boadicea   4 F5
Westminster Bridge SW1. Thornycroft, unveiled 1902. It

shows the famous British queen riding with her daughters in a chariot.

Charles I   4 F4
Trafalgar Sq SW1. Hubert le Sueur, 1675. Ordered to be destroyed in 1649, buried and kept safe until the Restoration in 1660. Royal Stuart Society lays a wreath here on the anniversary of his death, 30 January.

Sir Charles Chaplin   4 E3
Leicester Sq WC2. Doubleday, unveiled 1981 by the actor Sir Ralph Richardson. With his customary bowler hat and walking stick, he is appropriately surrounded by cinemas.

Sir Winston Churchill   4 F5
Parliament Sq SW1. 1973 by Ivor Roberts-Jones. Magnificent bronze statue of one of Britain's greatest statesmen, in naval overcoat, half-facing the House of Commons.

Oliver Cromwell   4 F6
Old Palace Yard SW1. Bronze by Thornycroft 1899. Holds a Bible in one hand and sword in the other. Paid for by Prime Minister Lord Rosebery as Parliament refused. Significantly, he stands with his back to the House of Parliament!

Elizabeth I   5 B2
St Dunstan-in-the-West, Fleet St EC4. Cast during the Queen's lifetime, 1586, by Kerwin. Originally stood over Lud Gate.

Eros   4 E3
Piccadilly Circus W1. Gilbert 1893. London's first aluminium statue, officially representing the Angel of Christian Charity. Paid for by public donations and restored in 1984.

Sir Thomas More   5 B2
Carey St WC2. Stone figure by Smith 1866. More was 'the faithful servant both of God and the King. Martyred 5 July 1535'.

Peter Pan   3 E4
Kensington Gardens W2. Frampton 1912. Delightful figure of the fictional fairy character. Erected overnight as a surprise for the children. Carved animals at the base have been worn away by the strokes of tiny hands.

Captain Scott   4 E4
Waterloo Place SW1. Bronze by Lady Scott, erected 1915, of her husband in full arctic kit.

Victoria Memorial   4 D5
In front of Buckingham Palace SW1. By Brock, 1911. Impressive memorial to Queen Victoria which includes a fine, dignified figure of the Queen, the best of many statues of her.

Duke of Wellington   4 B5
Hyde Park Corner SW1. Huge bronze figure by J.E. Boehm (1888) of the Duke astride his favourite horse, Copenhagen. He looks towards Apsley House (now the Wellington Museum) where he lived.

Commemorative plaques

Since 1866, blue plaques have been used to mark houses and other buildings associated with famous people or events. There are now nearly 400 of them commemorating the lives of architects, artists, composers, politicians, scientists, soldiers and writers. The following are a selection:

Baden-Powell, Robert Stephenson   **3 D5**
Founder of the Boy Scouts movement. Lived at 9 Hyde Park Gate SW7.

Berlioz, Hector   **4 C1**
Composer. Stayed at 58 Queen Anne St W1.

Bligh, William   **4 C2**
Captain of HMS *Bounty*. Lived at 17 South Molton St W1.

Browning, Elizabeth Barrett   **4 A1**
Poet and wife of poet Robert Browning. Lived at 99 Gloucester Place W1.

Brunel, Isambard Kingdom   **6 D5**
Civil engineer. Lived at 98 Cheyne Walk SW3.

Engels, Friedrich   **1 B2**
Political philosopher and novelist. Lived at 121 Regent's Park Rd NW1.

Gwynne, Nell   **4 E4**
Actress, mistress of Charles II. Lived at 79 Pall Mall SW1.

Handel, George Frideric   **4 C3**
Composer and musician. Lived and died at 25 Brook St W1.

Kipling, Rudyard   **4 F4**
Poet and story writer. Lived at 43 Villiers St WC2.

Marconi, Guglielmo Marchese   **3 B2**
Inventor and pioneer of wireless communication. Lived at 71 Hereford Rd W2.

Mozart, Wolfgang Amadeus   **7 A2**
Composer and musician. Composed his first symphony at 180 Ebury St SW1.

Pepys, Samuel   **5 C2**
Diarist. Born in a house on the site of Salisbury Court EC4.

Shaw, George Bernard   **2 E5**
Dramatist and essayist. Lived at 29 Fitzroy Sq W1.

Scott, Captain Robert Falcon   **6 E4**
Antarctic explorer. Lived at 56 Oakley St SW3, from where he left on his last fatal journey.

Turner, Joseph Mallord William   **6 D5**
Painter. Lived at 119 Cheyne Walk SW3.

Wilde, Oscar Fingall O'Flahertie   **6 F4**
Poet, dramatist and wit. Lived at 34 Tite St SW3.

Wren, Sir Christopher   **5 D3**
Architect. Lived at 49 Bankside SE1.

ANNUAL EVENTS

London plays host to a vast number of annual events, from colourful ceremonies to more obscure London customs such as the Doggett's Coat & Badge Race. For exact dates, times and places, where not given, contact one of the Information Centres (see p19).

Daily ceremonies

Contact the London Tourist Board Information Centre, Victoria Station Forecourt SW1. (071-730 3488) for further information.

Ceremony of the Keys   **5 G3**

HM Tower of London, Tower Hill EC3. 071-709 0765. The Chief Warder of the Yeomen Warders, with an escort from the Brigade of Guards, locks the West Gates, the Middle Tower and Byward Tower. Listen out for the words spoken every night for 700 years – 'Halt! Who comes there?' 'The keys.' 'Whose keys?' 'Queen Elizabeth II's keys.' 'Pass the keys. All's well.' *21.40 Mon-Sun by written application, well in advance and enclosing a stamped addressed envelope, to the Governor, Queen's House, HM Tower of London EC3.* Free.

Changing the Guard   **4 D5**

Buckingham Palace SW1. Takes place inside the palace railings and in *summer* the crowds makes it difficult to see much. The custom began in the days when the Life Guards were responsible for protecting the life of the monarch. An alternative is to see the Guards on their way from Chelsea or Wellington Barracks. They leave Chelsea at *10.45* and Wellington at *11.00.* The palace ceremony takes place at *11.30 every day in summer, alternate days in winter.*

Also at **St James's Palace (4 D4)** at *11.15*; **Whitehall (4 F4)** at *11.00 Mon-Sat, 10.00 Sun,* leaving Hyde Park Barracks *10.38 Mon-Sat, 09.39 Sun;* and **Windsor Castle**, Windsor, Berks (0753) 868286 at *11.00-11.30 every day in summer, alternate days in winter.* Free.

Other daily events

Speakers' Corner   **4 A3**

Marble Arch corner of Hyde Park. A remaining vestige of the British tradition of free speech is this institution of impromptu discourses by unknown orators, usually on religion or politics.

Most lively on *Sun*. Also at Lincoln's Inn Fields (**5 A2**) and Tower Hill (**5 G3**) *Mon-Fri lunchtime*. Free.

Feeding the pigeons   **4 F4**

Trafalgar Sq WC2. A famous tradition. You will soon find yourself accosted by touts who want to sell you bird-seed and photographs of yourself. Beware, if you buy any seed, the pigeons are likely to land on your head!

Annual events

JANUARY

International Boat Show   **6 A3**

Earl's Court Exhibition Centre, Warwick Rd SW5. 071-385 1200. The latest pleasure crafts, yachts and equipment to marvel at. Largest boat show in Europe. *Early Jan*. Charge.

January sales

Most stores have stock-clearing sales after the Christmas shopping spree. Some fantastic bargains to be had, especially at Harrods, but these go quickly and there are always huge crowds, so get there early. The real fanatics camp outside the stores, sometimes for days beforehand in a bid to be first in.

Lord Mayor of Westminster's New Year's Day   **4 D4**
Parade

Information: 081-992 9600. One of the largest parades in Europe, with some 5000 performers. Marching bands, colourful floats and veteran vehicles. Starts at Piccadilly and ends at Hyde Park (**4 B4**) where the entertainment continues. *1 Jan*. Free.

Royal Epiphany Gifts   **4 D4**

Chapel Royal, St James's Place, Marlborough Rd SW1. Picturesque ceremony involving two 'Gentlemen Ushers' offering gold, frankincense and myrrh on behalf of the Queen. *Admission by ticket only, apply to the above address. 11.30, 6 Jan*. Free.

FEBRUARY

Chinese New Year Festival   **4 E3**

Chinatown, Gerrard St W1. Noisy, colourful affair in the heart of the West End to celebrate Chinese New Year. Papier-mâché dragons, extravagant costumes and brightly-lit festivities animate the whole area. 1992 is the Year of the Monkey and 1993 the Year of the Rooster. *Jan or Feb*. Free.

Soho Pancake Day Race   **4 D3**

Carnaby St W1. Information: 071-287 0907. Pancakes are the traditional food eaten on Shrove Tuesday, the day before the beginning of Lent. Watch various teams running with frying pans and tossing their pancakes as they go. *End Feb or during Mar, depending on when Easter falls*. Free.

MARCH

Chelsea Antiques Fair   6 E3
Chelsea Old Town Hall, King's Rd SW3. 071-352 3619. Good selection of antiques and antiquities, with some real bargains. *Mid Mar.*

John Stow Memorial Service   5 F2
Church of St Andrew Undershaft, St Mary Axe EC3. The Lord Mayor attends this commemoration of London's first historian and places a new quill pen in the hand of Stow's statue. *11.30 Sun in Mar or Apr.* Free.

Oxford v. Cambridge Boat Race
River Thames, Putney SW15 to Mortlake SW14. The annual rowing challenge between the dark and light blues (Oxford and Cambridge universities) has taken place since 1845. Plenty of vantage points from bridges, banks or riverside pubs – advisable to get there early for a good view. *Sat afternoon in Mar or Apr.* Free.

APRIL

Easter Sunday Parade   6 F5
Battersea Park SW11. Colourful carnival procession including jugglers, stilt walkers and marching bands. Fun fair and other entertainments. *15.00 Easter Sun.* Free.

London Harness Horse Parade   1 C4
Regent's Park NW1. Fine breeds from Shires and Somersets to lighter-weight horses and ponies, carts, brewer's vans and drays are paraded around the Inner Circle at *12.00.* Judging starts at *09.30* and the public can inspect the horses before the parade. *Easter Mon.* Free.

London Marathon
Information: 081-948 7935. The world's largest road race with competitors a mixture of international marathon runners, serious runners, joggers, celebrities and fancy dress 'fun' runners (usually raising money for charity). Good atmosphere with large crowds at both the start (Greenwich Park SE10) and finish (Westminster Bridge SW1 – **4 F5**). *Late Apr.* Free to spectators.

Tower of London Church Parade   5 G3
Tower of London, Tower Hill EC3. 071-709 0765. The Yeomen Warders, in state dress, are inspected and parade before and after morning service at *11.00 Easter Sun.* Free.

MAY

Chelsea Flower Show   7 A3
Chelsea Royal Hospital, Royal Hospital Rd SW3. 071-834 4333. Recorded information: 071-828 1744. Superb floral displays burst into bloom in the grounds of the Royal Hospital. Exhibitions include extravagant landscaped gardens, fruit and

vegetable   displays,   garden   equipment   and   other
green-fingered accessories. *For four days, third week of May.*
Charge.

FA Cup Final
Wembley Stadium, Wembley, Middx. 081-902 8833. Climax of
the English football season. *Some tickets from the above
number, but the majority go to the two clubs whose teams
are participating. Early May.* Charge.

Glyndebourne Festival Opera Season
Glyndebourne, nr Lewes, E. Sussex. (0273) 541111. Well-
heeled Londoners don evening dress to hear superlative
singing and dine out on the lawn, if the summer weather
permits! Performances *May-Aug.* Charge.

Open Air Art Exhibitions
Artists display their work for the public to view (and hopefully
buy!).
Victoria Embankment Gardens WC2 (**4 F4**) – *2-14 May & Mon-
Sat during Aug.*
Royal Ave, King's Rd SW3 (**6 F3**) – *May-Oct 11.00-18.00 Sat.*
Works are also displayed against the railings on the Green
Park side of Piccadilly (**4 C4**) and along Bayswater Road out-
side Kensington Gardens and Hyde Park (**3 D3**). *Sun morning
all year round.* Free.

Rugby League Challenge Cup Final
Wembley Stadium, Wembley, Middx. Climax of the English
Rugby League season, battled out in the mud at Wembley.
*Contact the Rugby Football League (0532) 623637 for details.
Late Apr/early May.* Charge.

JUNE
Beating the Retreat   4 F4
Horse Guards' Parade SW1. 071-839 6815. Colourful military
display of marching and drilling bands acknowledging the
'retreat' or setting of the sun. Evening floodlit performances
especially delightful. *For tickets phone 071-930 0292. Early
Jun.* Charge.

Derby Day
Epsom Racecourse, Epsom, Surrey. (0373) 726311. World-
famous flat horserace. Also a fun fair and side shows. *1st
week in Jun.* Charge.

Election of the Sheriffs of the City of London   5 D2
Guildhall EC2. 071-606 3030. Lord Mayor and Aldermen of the
City of London take part in a colourful ceremony. Tradition
dictates that posies are carried to ward off 'the plague'.
Midsummer's Day, unless it falls on a Sat or Sun. Free.

Founder's Day   7 A3
Chelsea Royal Hospital, Royal Hospital Rd SW3. 071-730

0161. Chelsea pensioners parade in their colourful uniforms for inspection, sometimes by royalty. *Early Jun*. Free.

The Garter Ceremony
St George's Chapel, Windsor, Berks. Service dating from 14thC attended by the Queen. Preceded by procession with the Household Cavalry and Yeomen of the Guard. *Mon afternoon of Ascot week (usually 3rd week in Jun)*. Free.

Kenwood Lakeside Concerts
Kenwood House, Hampstead Lane NW3. 071-973 3427. Bookings: 071-379 4444. Classical concerts beside Kenwood Lake on Hampstead Heath performed by some of the most famous orchestras in the world. Often end with a spectacular firework displays. *Sat evenings Jun-Aug*. Charge.

Lord's Test Match
Lord's Cricket Ground, St John's Wood Rd NW8. 071-289 1611/5. Recorded information on state of play: 071-289 8011. Although confusing for the beginner, cricket is a British institution. The Test Match takes place here over *three or five days Jun or Jul*. Charge.

Royal Academy Summer Art Exhibition   4 D3
Royal Academy, Burlington House, Piccadilly W1. 071-439 7438. Aspiring Cézannes and Hockneys enter their works to be admired and hopefully bought! Huge mixture of styles from amateur-looking oils to beautifully-crafted architectural designs. Be prepared for long queues. *Jun-mid Aug*. Charge.

Royal Ascot Races
Ascot Racecourse, Ascot, Berks. (0344) 22211. Famous event where hats and horses vie for attention. The Queen and other members of the royal party travel the course in open carriages each day before the race. *Three days – usually 3rd week in Jun*. Charge.

Trooping the Colour
Colourful pageant and procession to celebrate the Queen's official birthday. Royal party leaves Buckingham Palace (**4 D5**) at around *10.30* and proceeds along the Mall (**4 D5**) to Horse Guards' Parade (**4 F4**), then to Whitehall (**4 F4**) and back again. *Tickets awarded by ballot from The Brigade Major, Trooping the Colour, Household Division, Horse Guards' Parade SW1 (enclose a stamped addressed envelope). 11.00 Sat nearest 11 Jun*. Charge.

Wimbledon Lawn Tennis Championships
Church Rd SW19. Recorded information: 081-946 2244. Height of the tennis circuit tournaments and one of the most famous championships in the world. Early evening is the best time to go to avoid the crowds. *Tickets for Centre Court, No.1 and No.2 Court are awarded by public ballot, but you can queue for tickets for the other courts on the day of play. 14.00 Mon-Sat. Last week Jun & first week Jul*. Charge.

JULY
City of London Festival
Information: 071-377 0540/248 4260. Arts festival held in the
Barbican (**5 D1**), the Tower of London (**5 G3**), Mansion House
(**5 E2**), St Paul's Cathedral (**5 D2**), many fine churches and the
City's open spaces. Concerts, opera, exhibitions, poetry,
drama, dance, jazz and many varied street events. *Three
weeks in Jul.* Some events free, some charge.
Doggett's Coat & Badge Race
Information: 071-626 3531. London Bridge (**5 E4**) to Chelsea
Bridge (**7 B4**). Started 1715 to commemorate the accession of
King George I. Sometimes called the 'Watermen's Derby',
after the men who used to rule London's transport on the
Thames, it is limited to six recently-qualified watermen.
Colourful and fun event. *Late Jul.* Free.
Henley Royal Regatta
Henley-on-Thames, Oxon. (0491) 572153. Steeped in tradition,
where smart outfits and even smarter picnics try to outdo
each other on the bank whilst watching the skilled rowers do
their stuff. *For exact dates phone the above number. Early Jul.*
Free in public areas.
Proms (Henry Wood Promenade Concerts)   **3 E5**
Royal Albert Hall, Kensington Gore SW7. 071-589 8212.
Classical music festival culminating in the famous Last Night
of the Proms at the Royal Albert Hall (see p51). *Late Jul until
Sep.* Charge.
Royal Tournament   **6 A3**
Earl's Court Exhibition Centre, Warwick Rd SW5. 071-373
8141. Impressive military spectacle presented by the armed
forces with much pageantry, military bands and daring feats.
Two weeks mid Jul. Charge.
Swan Upping
Information: 071-236 1863. London Bridge (**5 E4**) to Henley,
Berks. Ownership of the swans on the Thames is divided
between the Dyers' Company, the Vintners' Company and the
Sovereign. The Queen's Swan Keeper leads the keepers of the
other companies and the swanherds to a fleet of boats, banners
flying, for the trip up the reaches from London as far as Henley
for the swan census. The cygnets are branded by nicking their
beaks – one nick for the Dyers'; two for the Vintners'; the
Sovereign's are left unmarked. *Phone in advance to find out
exactly where the fleet is at any one time. Jul-Aug.* Free.

AUGUST
Notting Hill Carnival   **3 A3**
Ladbroke Grove and Notting Hill W11. Started originally as a
celebration of West Indian culture, a lively, noisy, colourful
event with music, dancing in the streets and processions. *Sun*

is children's day, and the main processions take place on *Bank hol Mon. Last Mon in Aug.* Free.

SEPTEMBER
Election of Lord Mayor of London 5 D2
St Lawrence Jewry, Gresham St EC2 to the Guildhall EC2. 071-606 3030. Colourful procession to celebrate the election of the new Lord Mayor of London. *Michaelmas Day.* Free.

Last Night of the Proms 3 E5
Royal Albert Hall, Kensington Gore SW7. 071-589 8212. The culmination of the Proms concerts. Traditional rousing performance of *Land of Hope and Glory. Tickets by qualification system only – contact the above address. Mid Sep.* Charge.

OCTOBER
Her Majesty's Judges & Queen's Counsels 4 F6
Annual Breakfast
After a special service at Westminster Abbey, there is a procession to the House of Lords for the opening of the Law Term. *1 Oct.* Free.

Horse of the Year Show
Wembley Arena, Wembley, Middx. 081-902 8833. Fine showjumping with many of the world-famous competitors under one roof. *Early Oct.* Charge.

NOVEMBER
Admission of the Lord Mayor Elect 5 D2
Guildhall EC2. 071-606 3030. The Lord Mayor takes office. Colourful ceremony including the handing over of insignia by the former Lord Mayor. *Fri before Lord Mayor's Show. Mid Nov.* Free.

Christmas lights 4 D2
Oxford St and Regent St W1. Bright and imaginative illuminations line the streets and shop windows to celebrate the season. Ceremoniously switched on in *early Nov.* Free.

Guy Fawkes Day
Bonfires are lit all over London and Britain to commemorate the discovery of the Gunpowder Plot of 1605, by which Guy Fawkes and his fellow conspirators intended to blow up James I and Parliament. Organised public events are the safest and usually the most spectacular. *Evening 5 Nov.* Charge for organised displays.

London to Brighton Veteran Car Run 3 G4
Serpentine Rd, Hyde Park W2. Information: 081-686 2525. First held on 'Emancipation Day' in 1896 which celebrated the abolition of the Act stipulating that a car must be preceded by a person walking with a red flag at 2 miles per hour. A colourful event with the contestants in period costume, only open to

cars made before 1905. They start at *08.00* and aim to reach Brighton by *16.00. First Sun in Nov*. Free.

Lord Mayor's Procession & Show

The newly-elected Lord Mayor is driven in the 1756 State Coach, with a procession of about 140 floats, from the Guildhall (**5 D2**) to the Law Courts (**5 B2**) to be received and sworn in by the Lord Chief Justice. Biggest ceremonial event in the City. *11.10 second Sat in Nov*. Free.

Remembrance Sunday   **4 F5**

The Cenotaph, Whitehall SW1. Service attended by the Queen and the Prime Minister to honour the dead of both World Wars. Takes place at the eleventh hour of the eleventh day (or nearest Sun) of the eleventh month – the anniversary of the armistice of World War I. Poppies sold in the street to raise money for ex-servicemen. Get there early for a good view. *11.00 Sun nearest 11 Nov*. Free.

State Opening of Parliament

The Queen, in the Irish State Coach, is driven from Buckingham Palace (**4 D5**) to the House of Lords (**4 F5**) to open Parliament after the summer recess. Good views from the north side of The Mall – get there early. *10.30 1st week Nov*. Free.

DECEMBER

Annual Ice Show

Wembley Arena, Wembley, Middx. 081-902 8833. A spectacular and colourful pantomime on ice. Good family entertainment. *Dec-Mar*. Charge.

Carol services   **4 F6**

Westminster Abbey, Broad Sanctuary SW1. 071-222 7110. Carol services on *26, 27 & 28 Dec*. Free.

Carol singing   **4 F4**

Trafalgar Sq WC2. Carols are recorded on tape so you can just listen or sing along! *All through Dec*. Free.

Christmas Tree   **4 F4**

Trafalgar Sq WC2. Each year the citizens of Oslo donate a Norwegian spruce (a custom dating from World War II). It is brightly lit from *16.00* and carols are sung around it. *Mid Dec-6 Jan (Twelfth Night)*. Free.

New Year's Eve   **4 F4**

Trafalgar Sq WC2. Thousands gather in the square to bring in the New Year with massed singing of *Auld Lang Syne* and dancing round the fountains. Listen out for Big Ben tolling midnight. *31 Dec*. Free.

Tower of London Church Parade   **5 G3**

Tower of London, Tower Hill EC3. 071-709 0765. The Yeomen Warders, in state dress, are inspected and parade before and after morning service. *11.00 Sun before Xmas*. Free.

MUSEUMS & GALLERIES

London's national museums and galleries contain some of the richest treasures in the world, from stamps to temples, collected during British explorations around the world. They range from the vast British Museum to more recent and specialist additions and many now incorporate interactive displays and exhibits. Apart from the national art collections in the Tate Gallery, the National Gallery and the National Portrait Gallery, London is further enriched by other, once private, collections, now open to the public. It has long been a tradition that national museums and galleries are free, but some have now found it necessary to introduce either voluntary contributions or a fixed admission fee. Special exhibitions usually incur an entrance fee.

Bank of England Museum   5 E2

Bank of England, Threadneedle St EC2. Charts the Bank's history from 1694 to the high-tech world of modern banking. Houses unique English banknotes, gold bars and the Bank's silver collection. *Open Easter-Sep 10.00-17.00 Mon-Fri, 11.00-17.00 Sat, Sun & Bank hols; Oct-Easter 10.00-17.00 Mon-Fri only.* Free.

HMS Belfast   5 F4

Symons Wharf, Vine Lane SE1. 071-407 6434. The largest battle cruiser ever built for the Royal Navy, now a permanent museum showing its role during wartime. Film shows and lectures. *Open Oct-Mar 10.00-16.30 Mon-Sun; Apr-Sep 10.00-18.30 Mon-Sun.* Charge.

British Museum   1 G6

Great Russell St WC1. 071-636 1555. The world's greatest collection of antiquities and the national collection of archaeology and ethnography with four million (or so!) objects ranging from pre-historic to modern. Pick up a copy of the free information map at the entrance to help you plan your way around. Highlights include the Rosetta Stone; Roman pavements (Room 16); the Elgin marbles (Room 8); 'Pete Marsh', the 2000-year-old murdered Lindow man found preserved in a Cheshire bog (Room 35); and the Sutton Hoo treasures from the burial site of a 7thC Anglo-Saxon king (Room 41). Also famous for mummies including those of humans, cats, crocodiles and even baboons. Domed Reading Room (1857) where Karl Marx studied and wrote *Das Kapital (open to members only)*. Next to the main hall is the **British Library** which contains, by law, one copy of every book, periodical or newspaper printed in Great Britain. Collection includes two of the four Magna Cartas, the Lindisfarne Gospels and Shakespeare's first folio. Restaurant. Café. Excellent shop. *Guided tours (1½ hrs) at 10.30, 11.00, 13.30 & 14.00 Mon-Sat, 14.45, 15.15 & 15.45 Sun. (Charge).* Museum *open 10.00-17.00 Mon-Sat, 14.30-18.00 Sun.* Free (charge for special exhibitions).

Cabinet War Rooms   **4 F5**
Clive Steps, King Charles St SW1. 071-930 6961. Intriguing underground suite of 19 rooms used by Winston Churchill and his War Cabinet from August 1939-September 1945 as a meeting, planning and information centre. See Winston's bedroom and the desk from which he made some of his famous war-time broadcasts. *Personal sound guide included in entrance fee. Open 10.00-17.15 Mon-Sun.* Charge.

Commonwealth Institute   **3 B6**
230 Kensington High St W8. 071-603 4535. Near the grand gates of Holland Park, founded in 1887 to promote knowledge of Queen Victoria's Empire. Fun, friendly and lively, with lots of interactive and often humorous displays to show the history, people, landscapes, wildlife and crafts of the Commonwealth. Restaurant. Shop. *Open 10.00-17.00 Mon-Sat, 12.00-17.00 Sun.* Free.

Courtauld Institute Galleries   **4 G3**
Somerset House, Strand WC2. 071-872 0220. Notable assembly of paintings, furniture and drawings from six private collections. Fine examples of baroque furniture, Flemish and Italian Old Masters, the Mark Gambier-Parry Bequest and works by Manet, Renoir, Cézanne, van Gogh and Gauguin. *Open 10.00-18.00 Mon-Sat, 14.00-18.00 Sun.* Charge.

Design Museum   **5 G4**
Butler's Wharf, Shad Thames SE1. 071-403 6933. Founded by Sir Terence Conran, the aim is to make everyone aware of design past, present and future through a number of provocative exhibits. Furniture, gadgets and graphics from cars to tea-pots. Blueprint Café renowned for good food. Bookshop, library. *Tours by prior arrangement. Open 11.30-18.30 Tue-Sun. Closed Mon except Bank hols.* Charge.

Dulwich Picture Gallery
College Rd, Dulwich SE21. 081-693 5254. The first public art gallery in England (1814). Includes works by Claude, Cuyp, Rembrandt (including his portrait of Jacob II de Gheyn – stolen four times), Rubens, van Dyck, Gainsborough, Hogarth, Canaletto and Watteau. Shop. *Guided tour 15.00 Sun (included*

in entrance fee). Open 10.00-13.00 & 14.00-17.00 Tue-Fri, 10.00-17.00 Sat, 14.00-17.00 Sun. Closed Mon. Charge.

Geffrye Museum

Kingsland Rd, Hackney E2. 071-739 9893. Housed in several early 18thC almshouses, exhibitions of the British living room from Tudor times to the 1950s including the pre-fabs of the 1940s, a panelled Elizabethan Room, an early Georgian Room and two stylish 1930s rooms. Café. Shop. Gardens. *Open 10.00-17.00 Tue-Sat, 14.00-17.00 Sun.* Free.

Hayward Gallery 5 A4

South Bank Centre SE1. 071-928 3144. Main venue for large-scale temporary exhibitions of both historical and contemporary art from America, Europe and Britain. Shop. *Open 10.00-18.00 Mon-Sun, (to 20.00 Tue-Wed). Closed between exhibitions.* Charge.

Imperial War Museum 5 B6

Lambeth Rd SE1. 071-416 5000. Popular museum concentrating equally on the human as well as the mechanical side of war. Vast collection of tanks, weapons and aircraft including a Mark I Spitfire. The Blitz Experience lets you feel, see and hear what it was like to be in London during the bombing of the 1940s. Operation Jericho is a flight simulator allowing you to experience flying with the RAF to release captured Resistance fighters. Good café. Shop. *Open 10.00-18.00 Mon-Sun.* Charge.

Institute of Contemporary Arts (ICA) 4 E4

Nash House, The Mall SW1. 071-930 3647. Three galleries with changing contemporary art exhibitions. Widely regarded as one of the most innovative art venues in the country. Also two cinemas, a theatre and video library. Restaurant. Café/bar. Bookshop. Galleries *open 12.00-22.00 Mon-Fri, 12.00-20.00 Sat & Sun.* Charge.

Jewish Museum 1 F5

Woburn House, Tavistock Sq WC1. 071-388 4525. Anglo-Jewish life, its history and traditions illustrated by ceremonial and ritual objects. *Open 10.00-16.00 (last admission 15.45). Closed Mon, Sat & Jewish hols.* Donation requested.

London Planetarium 1 C5

Marylebone Rd NW1. 071-486 1121. Mind-boggling journey amongst the stars, space and cosmos! Thousands of projected images become clear with an expert guide to explain the astronomical mysteries. *Open Apr-Oct 10.40-17.20 Mon-Sun; Nov-Mar 12.40-17.20 Mon-Fri, 10.40-17.20 Sat & Sun.* Charge (combined entrance ticket with Madame Tussaud's available).

London Toy & Model Museum 3 D3

21 Craven Hill W2. 071-262 9450. Vast collection of dolls, model cars, tin soldiers and countless other toys, spanning

over 100 years. Also model railway and carousel ride. Café. *Open 10.00-17.30 Mon-Sat, 11.00-17.30 Sun.* Charge.

London Transport Museum   **4 G3**
39 Wellington St WC2. 071-379 6344. Story of London's passenger transport system told through moving and static exhibits. 'Drive' modern-day tubes and buses and work the points and signals in a tunnel. Be prepared for queues. Shop. *Open 10.00-18.00 (last admission 17.15) Mon-Sun.* Charge.

Madame Tussaud's   **1 C5**
Marylebone Rd NW1. 071-935 6861. To number among the waxwork figures here is proof of fame! Meet Bob Geldof, the Royal Family, the Beatles, Mrs Thatcher and Joan Collins alongside a galaxy of stars from all walks of life. Murderers lurk in the Chamber of Horrors, which harbours evil-looking villains and stories of murder most foul. There's also a reconstruction of the gun deck of HMS *Victory* at the height of battle – bangs, smoke, screams and all. Very busy – be prepared for queues. Café. *Open 10.00-17.30 Mon-Fri, 09.30-17.30 Sat & Sun.* Charge (combined ticket with London Planetarium available).

Museum of London   **2 E6**
150 London Wall EC2. 071-600 3699. London's biography from pre-history to present day with a variety of costumes and archaeological finds. Reconstructions include a Roman kitchen, the devastation of the Great Fire in 1666, a ghoulish cell from Newgate Prison, and Selfridges' 1920s art deco lifts. Restaurant. Shop. *Open 10.00-18.00 Tue-Sat, 12.00-18.00 Sun. Closed Mon except Bank hols.* Charge.

Museum of Mankind   **4 D3**
6 Burlington Gdns W1. 071-437 2224. Ethnographic Department of the British Museum. Contains the world's largest and best collection of artefacts, clothing and housing from areas in the Americas, Oceania and Africa. *Open 10.00-17.00 Mon-Sat, 14.30-18.00 Sun.* Free.

Museum of the Moving Image (MOMI)   **5 B4**
South Bank SE1. 071-928 3535. The story of moving images from Chinese shadow theatre to film, television and satellite. Actors and presenters help you to read the news or animate a cartoon. Frequently changing displays and plenty of moving exhibits. Restaurant. Bar. Shop. *Open 10.00-18.00 (last admission 17.00) Mon-Sun.* Charge.

National Gallery   **4 F3**
Trafalgar Sq WC2. 071-839 3321. The nation's major collection of historical paintings, founded in 1824, covering European schools from the 13thC to 20thC. A leaflet, available at the entrance, leads you to the 16 most famous paintings. Daily tours also highlight selected works. Famous painters include

Rembrandt, Rubens, Frans Hals, van Dyck, Velazquez, El Greco, Cézanne, Monet and van Gogh. The Sainsbury Wing, opened in 1990, houses a collection of early Renaissance paintings including works by Botticelli, Raphael and Titian with great attention paid to the display of the paintings as well as the works themselves. Restaurant. Café/bar. Shop. *Regular guided tours every day (contact the information desk for times). Open 10.00-18.00 Mon-Sat, 14.00-18.00 Sun.* Free.

National Maritime Museum

Romney Rd, Greenwich SE10. 081-858 4422. In a beautiful riverside setting and incorporating the Old Royal Observatory and Queen's House, this is the world's largest collection of boats and navigational instruments. Ships' models, carved figureheads, weapons, pictures and fine silver collections tell the story of Britain and the sea, its navy, merchants and explorers. *Open Apr-Sep 10.00-18.00 Mon-Sat, 14.00-18.00 Sun; Oct-Mar 10.00-17.00 Mon-Sat, 14.00-17.00 Sun.* Charge.

National Portrait Gallery   **4 F3**

2 St Martin's Place WC2. 071-306 0055. The former stipulation that for inclusion in the National Portrait Gallery you had to be dead has now been relaxed! Start on the fifth floor and work your way down for a comprehensive, chronological look at portraits of the famous and infamous from Richard II to Mick Jagger via Nell Gwynne, William Shakespeare, Winston Churchill and the present Royal Family. Special exhibitions on famous people in the arts, sciences, politics and armed forces; also sculptures, miniatures, drawings and caricatures. Café. Bookshop. *Open 10.00-16.00 Mon-Fri, 10.00-18.00 Sat, 14.00-18.00 Sun.* Free.

National Postal Museum   **5 D2**

King Edward Bldgs, King Edward St EC1. 071-239 5420. Thousands of stamps, stamp books and the Penny Black (which is not the rarest stamp they possess) franked as the world's first stamp on May 6 1840. *Open 09.30-16.30 Mon-Thur, to 16.00 Fri.* Free.

Natural History Museum & Geological Museum   **6 D1**

Cromwell Rd SW7. 071-938 9123. The Natural History Museum incorporates the Geological Museum, and displays a full range of exhibitions featuring the earth itself, known as the Earth Galleries of the Natural History Museum. Advanced and innovative methods of display involve, interest and entertain visitors of all ages. Special effects include a simulated earthquake experience. Among the most impressive sights is the massive skeleton of one of the largest land animals, Diplodocus, as well as the life-size model of a 90ft (27.5m) blue whale. The New Dinosaur exhibition, opened in March 1992, looks at every aspect of how dinosaurs lived and died, with large specimens and models. Restaurant. Café. Shop.

Both *open 10.00-18.00 Mon-Sat, 11.00-18.00 Sun.* Charge (free *16.30-18.00 Mon-Fri, 17.00-18.00 Sun & Bank hols*).

Public Record Office   **5 B2**
Chancery Lane WC2. 081-876 3444. Public records from the Norman invasion to the latest census, along with treaties, writs and state papers. Star attraction is the *Domesday Book*, a detailed survey of England in 1086. To trace your roots go to St Catharine's House, 10 Kingsway WC2 (071-242 0262) where the registers of births, marriages and deaths are kept. *Open 10.00-16.45 Mon-Fri.* Free.

Queen's Gallery   **4 C5**
Buckingham Palace, Buckingham Palace Rd SW1. 071-930 4832. The only part of Buckingham Palace open to the public, containing exhibits selected from the Royal art collection, regarded as one of the world's finest. Works by Rembrandt, Vermeer, Rubens, Holbein and Canaletto, as well as Sèvres porcelain, stamps and drawings. Shop. *Open 10.00-17.30 Tue-Sat, 14.00-17.30 Sun & Mon (last admission 16.30).* Charge.

Royal Academy of Arts   **4 D3**
Burlington House, Piccadilly W1. 071-439 7438. Holds a series of important special-loan exhibitions throughout the year. Famous for its annual 'Summer Exhibition' which displays thousands of works by living artists for view and sale. Can get very crowded at weekends. Café. Good shop. *Open 10.00-18.00 Mon-Sun.* Charge.

Royal Air Force Museum
Grahame Park Way, Hendon NW9. 081-205 2266. The first national museum covering all aspects of the RAF and its predecessor, the RFC. There are 70 full size aircraft, displayed in hangars on a former wartime airfield. See the tiny Bleriot monoplane, Sopwith Camel, Spitfire, Vulcan, Wellington, Lancaster and others. The history of flight is told through equipment, paintings and documents and you can try your hand at piloting a low-flying Tornado in a simulator. The Battle of Britain Hall has British, German and Italian aircraft including Spitfires, Hurricanes and a Messerschmidt. Good restaurant. Shop. *Open 10.00-18.00 Mon-Sun.* Charge.

Science Museum   **6 D1**
Exhibition Rd SW7. 071-938 8000. One of the three great national museums covering science, technology and medicine. Includes many historic exhibits as well as more modern ones, like the command module of Apollo 10. Ranging from a tiny tea-making machine of 1904 to huge steam locomotives, these show how modern scientific and industrial man has emerged. Plenty of hands-on exhibits and interactive displays, especially in the Flight Lab near the Aeronautics Gallery (third

floor), and in the Launch Pad (first floor). On the fourth and fifth floors is the Wellcome Museum of the History of Medicine with exhibits covering human history from the neolithic age to the 1980s. *Open 10.00-18.00 Mon-Sat, 11.00-18.00 Sun.* Charge.

Shakespeare Globe Museum   **5 D4**
1 Bear Gdns, Bankside SE1. 071-928 6342. Permanent exhibition of Shakespearian Theatre in a converted warehouse on the site of the last bear-bating ring to be used in the capital. A working reconstruction of Shakespeare's first Globe Theatre, following the original designs of 1599, is being constructed 300ft (91m) away. Shop. *Open 10.00-17.00 Mon-Sat, 14.00-17.30 Sun.* Charge.

Sir John Soane's Museum   **5 A2**
13 Lincoln's Inn Fields WC1. 071-405 2107. Britain's smallest and most unusual national museum in the former home of Sir John Soane, one of England's most renowned and respected architects. Amongst the treasures are Hogarth's paintings the *Rake's Progress* and the *Election* series; antiquities, including the sarcophagus of Seti I (1370BC) found in the Valley of the Kings; and paintings by Turner, Watteau, Reynolds and Canaletto. *Guided tour 14.30 Sat. Open 10.00-17.00 Tue-Sat.* Charge.

Tate Gallery   **7 E2**
Millbank SW1. 071-821 1313. Named after sugar millionaire Sir Henry Tate, who donated his Victorian paintings as its foundation. It is both the museum of British art, with a collection from the 16thC to around 1900, and holder of the national collection of international modern art. Works range from Impressionist to present day with often controversial new exhibits. The Clore Gallery holds the permanent Turner Bequest, including 300 paintings and 20,000 drawings by J.M.W. Turner. Due to the size of its collection, the Tate operates a policy of annual rotation, as they can only show a percentage of the works at any one time. Thus the star attractions mentioned below may or may not be on display when you visit – *phone the gallery in advance to avoid disappointment.* You may see Hogarth's self-portrait, Constable's *Flatford Mill*, William Blake's illustrations for Milton's *Paradise Lost*, or works by Monet, Seurat, Cézanne, Degas, Picasso, Matisse, Mondrian and British painters such as David Hockney, Ben Nicolson, and Augustus and Gwen John. Restaurant. Café. Excellent shop. *Regular guided tours Mon-Fri (contact the information desk for times). Open 10.00-17.50 Mon-Sat, 14.00-17.50 Sun.* Free (charge for special exhibitions).

Theatre Museum   **4 F3**
1 Tavistock St WC2. 071-836 7891. A branch of the Victoria & Albert Museum, right in the heart of 'theatreland' and the

perfect place to discover the history of the English stage since the 17thC. Magnificent collection of playbills, programmes, prompt books, drawings, photos, models, costumes and props. Café. Shop. *Open 11.00-19.00 Tue-Sun.* Charge.

Tower Hill Pageant   **5 G3**

Tower Hill Terrace EC3. 071-709 0081. London's first 'dark ride' museum, telling the story of 2000 years of the City of London. Automated cars take you past life-like scenes depicting London's waterfront from early Roman settlements to the Blitz. Some of the most fascinating discoveries of recent archaeological waterfront excavations, dating from Roman, Saxon and medieval times, are also on display. Café. Shop. *Open Apr-Oct 09.30-17.30 Mon-Sun; Nov-Mar 09.30-16.30 Mon-Sun.* Charge.

Tower of London   **5 G3**

Tower Hill EC3. 071-709 0765. Several museums and the Crown Jewels in the Jewel House – gold and silver pieces, Royal orbs, sceptres and crowns and the biggest cut diamond in the world, the First Star of Africa. The White Tower houses the Royal Armouries – the largest collection of medieval and Tudor armour in Britain. The Lower Martin Tower holds instruments of torture and the executioner's block and axe. Shops. *Guided tours by Yeomen Warders every ½ hr (except in bad weather) last tour 15.30 Mar-Oct, 14.30 Nov-Feb (included in entrance fee). Open Mar-Oct 09.30-18.00 Mon-Sat, 14.00-18.00 Sun (last admission 17.00); Nov-Feb 09.30-17.00 (last admission 16.00) Mon-Sat.* Charge.

Victoria & Albert Museum   **6 D1**

Cromwell Rd SW7. 071-938 8500. National museum of art and design and the largest decorative arts museum in the world. An immense and wide-ranging collection; where else can you see a Raphael Cartoon and 1960s designer clothes under one roof? Advisable to get the booklet *100 Things to See* at the bookshop to show you round the important exhibits. Restaurant. Shop. *Open 10.00-17.50 Mon-Sat, 14.30-17.50 Sun.* Donation welcome.

Wallace Collection   **4 B1**

Hertford House, Manchester Sq W1. 071-935 0687. A private collection of outstanding works of art which was bequethed to the nation by Lady Wallace in 1897. Splendid representation of the French 17thC and 18thC artists, including paintings by Fragonard, Watteau and Boucher. Home to the *Laughing Cavalier* by Frans Hals and also works by Rembrandt, Titian, Rubens, Canaletto and Guardi. Important collections of French furniture, Sèvres porcelain, majolica, Limoges enamel and armour. Shop. *Tours by prior arrangement. Open 10.00-17.00 Mon-Sat, 14.00-17.00 Sun.* Free.

OUT AND ABOUT

London is well-endowed with parks, gardens, commons, forests and heathland. There are over 80 parks within 7 miles of the centre of London – all that remains of early London's natural surrounding countryside. Left by accident, gift, or longsighted social intention, they provide a welcome breathing space. The royal parks are still the property of the Crown and were originally the grounds of royal homes or palaces. All parks are free to enter, but there may be charges to use the facilities within. For more information on London's great outdoors consult Nicholson's Outdoor London *by Sarah Brown.*

Parks and open spaces

Alexandra Park
N22. 081-365 2121. 220 acres (90ha) including Alexandra Palace, burnt to the ground six days after it was built in 1873. Rebuilt in 1936, it was again severely damaged by fire in 1980 and is now a multi-purpose entertainments and exhibition centre. Excellent views. Café. Park *open 24 hrs Mon-Sun.* **Facilities**: animal enclosure, arboretum, boating lake, children's playground, conservation area, ice rink, pitch and putt, playing fields, ski slope.

Battersea Park   6 F5
SW11. 081-871 7530. 200-acre (81ha) park opened 1853 by Queen Victoria. Festival Pleasure Gardens laid out in 1951 to celebrate the Festival of Britain. London Peace Pagoda built 1985 by monks and nuns of the Japanese Buddhist order Nipponzan Myohoji. Based on ancient Indian and Japanese designs, it stands at 110ft (33.5m) and has a double roof. Park *open 24 hrs Mon-Sun.* Playing fields, athletics track, tennis courts *open 06.00-dusk.* **Facilities**: all-weather sports surface, athletics track, boating and fishing lake, botanical garden (greenhouse *open 09.30-dusk*), bowling green, children's zoo, deer park, floodlit football pitch, playing fields, tennis.

Blackheath
SE3. 081-305 1807. 275 acres (111.4ha) of open grassland – a prime site for kite-flying and watching the sunset. Good views from all directions, especially Point Hill. The scene for many sporting events. Occasional festivals and fairs at *Easter, spring and late summer Bank hols.* Park *open 24 hrs Mon-Sun.* **Facilities**: bowling, cricket, model boat sailing, soccer, tennis.

Crystal Palace Park

SE20. 081-778 7148. 70 acres (28.4ha) of park named after Paxton's 1851 Great Exhibition building, removed here from Hyde Park but burnt down in 1936. The vast, impressive ruins still remain, however. National Youth & Sports Centre opened 1964 with a stadium for 12,000 spectators. In amongst the boating lakes are 20 life-sized replicas of large prehistoric animals such as the iguanodon, megalosaurus, pterodactyl and primitive reptiles. Park *open 09.00-½hr before dusk Mon-Sun.* **Facilities**: adventure playground, boating and pedalos, children's zoo, dry ski slope, fishing, mini fair, mini stream train, pony & trap, sports centre.

Green Park   4 C5

SW1. 071-930 1793. Just that, no statues or lakes – just 53 acres (22ha) of grass and trees. A favourite for office workers at *lunchtime in summer. Open dawn-dusk Mon-Sun.*

Greenwich Park

SE10. 081-858 2608. A royal park, gaining its royal connections with Henry VIII whose favourite residence was Greenwich Palace (the Royal Naval College now occupies the site). Excellent panoramic views. 200 acres (81ha) with avenues sloping down to the Thames, lined with chestnut trees and 13 acres (5.3ha) of wooded deer park. The National Maritime Museum and Old Royal Observatory are within the park and the London Marathon starts from here in *spring.* Bandstand used in *summer.* Park *open Apr-Oct 05.00 (for pedestrians – 07.00 for traffic)-22.00 Mon-Sun; Nov-Mar 07.00-18.00 (or dusk) Mon-Sun.* **Facilities**: boating pool, children's playground, cricket, rugby, tennis.

Hampstead Heath

(including Kenwood, Golders Hill Park, Parliament Hill) NW3. 071-485 4491. Open and hilly with a feel of real countryside, 800 acres (324ha) of park and woods with fine views of London. Crowded on *Bank hols* with visitors to the famous fair and equally famous pubs, the Bull & Bush, Spaniard's Inn and Jack Straw's Castle. Open-air concerts at Kenwood in *summer.* Parliament Hill, 320ft (110m), is a good spot for kite-flying and excellent views. Heath *open 24 hrs Mon-Sun.* Kenwood and Golders Hill *closed at night.* **Facilities**: athletics track, boating and fishing lakes, children's zoo, cricket, football, grass skiing, horse-riding (permit holders only), open-air swimming in several ponds, putting green, rounders, rugby, tennis.

Hampton Court & Bushy Park

Middx. 081-977 1328. 2000 acres (810ha) of royal park, the formal gardens of the great Tudor palace, Hampton Court, with ancient courtyards, superb flower gardens, the famous Maze and the Great Vine planted in 1768. **Bushy Park** is natural parkland with an artificial plantation, aquatic plants and ponds. Two herds of deer, fallow and red, roam throughout. Both parks have many fine avenues including the mile-long Chestnut Avenue with the 'Diana' fountain in Bushy Park. Both parks *open 07.45-dusk Mon-Sun.*

Holland Park 3 A5

W8. 071-602 2226. Behind the bustle of Kensington High Street are 55 acres (22.3ha) of calm and secluded lawns and gardens with peacocks, peafowl and pheasants. Once the private garden of Holland House, the Dutch garden dates from 1812 with fine tulip displays, iris and rose gardens, a yucca lawn and the Orangery. Also a remarkable woodland of 28 acres (11.3ha) containing 3000 species of rare British trees and plants. Open-air theatre in *summer.* Café. Park *open 08.00-dusk.* Flower garden *open to 24.00 Mon-Sun and illuminated at night.* **Facilities**: adventure playground, cricket, football, putting green, squash, tennis.

Hyde Park 3 F4

W1. 071-262 5484. A royal park since 1536, once part of the forest used by Henry VIII for hunting wild boar and bulls. 360 acres (137.7ha) of parkland, walks, Rotten Row for horse-riders, and the Serpentine – a fine lake, created originally from six ponds, now used for boating and swimming. Serpentine Bridge by George Rennie, 1826. Speakers' Corner, where anyone can speak about anything, is near Marble Arch – public executions were held at the Tyburn gallows, where Marble Arch now stands, until 1783. There are two good open-air cafés/restaurants, The Dell and the New Serpentine overlooking the lake (near the bridge). Baseball and softball are often played. Bandstand used in *summer.* Park *open 06.00-24.00 Mon-Sun.* The Lido *open May-Sep & Bank hols 10.00-18.00.* Charge for swimming. **Facilities**: boating lake, children's playground, open-air swimming, tennis.

Kensington Gardens 3 D4

W8. 071-262 5484. A formal and elegant addition to Hyde Park. 75 acres (111.4ha) of royal park, containing William III's Kensington Palace, Queen Anne's Orangery, the peaceful 'Sunken Garden', the Round Pond, perfect for sailing model boats, and – on the south side – the magnificent Albert Memorial – the nation's monument to Queen Victoria's husband. The Broad Walk, originally flanked by ancient elms, is now replanted with fragrant limes and maples and the nearby 'Flower Walk' is home to birds such as woodpeckers, flycatchers and tree-creepers. Queen Caroline created both the Long Water (Peter Pan's statue is here) and the Serpentine by ordering the damming of the Westbourne River. Nothing so rowdy as football or cars are allowed here! Café. Park *open*

07.00-¹/₂hr before dusk Mon-Sun. **Facilities**: children's playground, model boat sailing.

Primrose Hill   **1 B2**

NW1. 112 acres (46.6ha) of open land. For anyone who conquers its 206ft (62.7m) the rewards are great with excellent panoramic views over London and a helpful table identifying some of the most prominent landmarks. Popular with duellists in the 19thC, the cleverest battles you'll see now are between kite flyers. *Open 24 hrs Mon-Sun.*

Regent's Park   **1 C3**

NW1. 071-486 7905. A royal park of 472 acres (191ha), originally part of Henry VIII's great hunting forest in the 16thC. The design (1812-26), by John Nash, is of great distinction. It forms two concentric circles – the Inner with gardens and Outer with Regency terraces and imposing gateways. Here you'll find London Zoo (under threat of closure at time of publication), the Regent's Canal, a fine boating lake with 30 species of bird, a bandstand, fragrant flower gardens and the very fine Queen Mary's Rose Garden. Also home to the golden-domed London Central Mosque. Open-air theatre. Restaurant. Cafés. Park *open 05.00 (or dawn)-dusk Mon-Sun.* **Facilities**: athletics track, baseball, boating lake, cricket, football, rugby, tennis.

Richmond Park

Surrey. 081-948 3209. The largest of the royal parks, created by Charles I in 1637. 2358 acres (954.2ha) of natural open parkland with spinneys and plantations, bracken and ancient oaks, and over 600 red and fallow deer. Fine views of the Thames Valley from White Lodge (once a royal residence, now home to the Royal Ballet School). Restaurant and café in Pembroke Lodge. Park *open 07.00-¹/₂hr before dusk (from 07.30 in winter) Mon-Sun.* **Facilities**: children's playground, fishing (permit needed) football, golf, riding.

St James's Park   **4 E5**

SW1. 071-930 1793. St James's is the oldest royal park, acquired by Henry VIII in 1532 and laid out in imitation 'Versailles' style by Charles II. An attractive setting, with fine promenades and walks, a romantic Chinese-style lake, bridge, and weeping willows. The bird sanctuary on Duck Island has magnificent pelicans and over 20 species of duck and goose. Good views of Buckingham Palace, the domes and spires of Whitehall and, to the south, Westminster Abbey. The Mall and Constitution Hill are frequently part of royal ceremonial occasions. Bandstand used in *summer. Open dawn-dusk Mon-Sun.*

Botanic gardens

Many parks also have living botanical collections. Holland Park has a good arboretum and others have rock gardens and extensive rosé gardens, of which Queen Mary Rose Garden in Regent's Park is an outstanding example. The following provide tranquillity in the midst of London:

Chelsea Physic Garden   **6 F4**

Royal Hospital Rd SW3. 071-352 5646. Founded 1673 by the Worshipful Society of Apothecaries, for the collection and study of plants with medicinal value. Botanical research still carried out here. Rockery made from Icelandic lava and old stone from the Tower of London and many fine trees including the biggest olive tree in Britain – 30ft (9.1m). *Open Apr-Oct 14.00-17.00 Wed & Sun. Other times by appointment only.* Charge.

Museum of Garden History   **7 F1**

St Mary-at-Lambeth, Lambeth Rd SE1. 071-261 1891. 17thC garden founded at St Mary-at-Lambeth church by the Tradescants. As gardeners to Charles I and Henrietta Maria, the father and son team brought many rare plants into this country, some of which can be seen in the churchyard. *Open 11.00-15.00 Mon-Fri, 10.30-17.00 Sun. Closed Sat.* Free.

Royal Botanic Gardens, Kew

Kew Rd, Richmond, Surrey. 081-940 1171. Superb botanic gardens of 300 acres (121.5ha), founded in 1759 by Princess Augusta. Within the grounds are thousands of flowers and trees plus hot-houses for orchids, palms, ferns, cacti and alpine plants. Lake, aquatic garden and 10-storey pagoda by Sir William Chambers (1760) and the magnificent curved glass Palm House and Temperate House, 1884-8, are by Decimus Burton. The scientific aspect was developed by its two directors Sir William and Sir Joseph Hooker. The 17thC Queen's Garden has a delightful formal rose-bed and the newest addition is the Princess of Wales Conservatory, housing exotic plants. Café. Gift shop. Gardens *open 09.30-18.30 Mon-Sat. Hot-houses open 10.00-18.30. These times vary slightly throughout the year – phone in advance to check.* Charge.

Cemeteries

London's cemeteries provide a fascinating insight into Victorian attitudes, with their impressive and often idiosyncratic monuments. Originally privately owned and regimentally planted out, several have since become overgrown and peaceful sanctuaries for wildlife.

Brompton   **6 B4**

Old Brompton Rd SW10. Behind busy Fulham Road, vast and full of ornamental Victorian marble tombs and memorials. Emmeline Pankhurst, the suffragette, was buried here in 1928. Free.

Highgate

Swain's Lane N6. 081-340 1834. Popular from the first as a

final resting place because of the good views of London from Highgate West Hill! Winding paths lead up to The Egyptian Avenue and Cedar of Lebanon. Amongst its famous residents are Karl Marx, the writer George Eliot, Sir Ralph Richardson, the actor, and the poet Christina Rossetti. Tom Sayers, the bare fisted prizefighter, is guarded by the effigy of his mastiff who was chief mourner at his funeral and attended the ceremony in his own carriage. The conservation of the native woodland and abundance of wild flowers and birds is due to the efforts of the 'Friends of Highgate Cemetery', who offer guided tours round the western section *Apr-Oct 12.00, 14.00, 16.00 Mon-Fri, on the hour 11.00-16.00 Sat & Sun; Nov-Mar 12.00, 14.00 & 15.00 Mon-Fri, on the hour 11.00-15.00 Sat & Sun.* Eastern section *open Easter-end Oct 10.00-17.00 Mon-Sun; Nov-Easter 10.00-16.00 Mon-Sun (closed during funerals).* Charge for tours.

Kensal Green

Harrow Rd W10. 081-969 0152. Plenty of admirable monuments and many mature native trees lining the curving avenues. Famous tombs include W.M. Thackeray and Anthony Trollope, Isambard Kingdom Brunel and his father Sir Marc Isambard Brunel and James Miranda Barry, the Inspector General of the Army Medical Department, who on death was found to be a woman. *Open 09.00-17.30 Mon-Sat (10.00-13.00 Bank hols), 10.00-17.30 Sun.* Free.

Walking tours

Citisights of London

213 Brooke Rd E5. 081-806 4325. Huge variety of walking tours throughout the year. Something for everyone with themes which include *London's Criminal Underworld, John Betjeman's London, 200 Years along the City Wall* and *The Great Fire, Plague and Civil War.* Most walks last around *2 hrs.* **Meeting place**: either at the Museum of London or a tube station. *Phone the above number for details.* Charge.

Historical Tours

3 Florence Rd, South Croydon, Surrey. 081-688 4019. Focuses on London's history and offers a range of themes from medieval times to the present. Cover areas as diverse as Mayfair and the East End, Hampstead and Docklands. Walks last around *2 hrs.* **Meeting place**: usually at a tube station. *Phone for further details.* Charge.

London Silver Jubilee Walkway

12-mile (19km) walkway created for the Queen's Silver Jubilee in 1977. Circles the centre of London, passing close to many famous and historic buildings. Start at Leicester Square (**4 E3**)

and follow the discs set in the pavement. Leaflet obtainable
from the London Tourist Board, 26 Grosvenor Gdns SW1 (**7
B1**). 071-730 3488.

Perfect London Walks
P.O. Box 1708 NW6. 071-435 6413. Varied walks through
London including *Discovering London*, covering Bloomsbury,
Soho, Mayfair and Highgate; *Dickens' London*, tours around
the old Jewish quarter and several pub walks, which take
slightly longer than the *2 hrs* you should allow for the others!
Meeting place: usually at a tube station. *Phone for further
details*. Charge.

Tour Guides International
2 Bridge St SW1. 071-839 2498/5314. Choose from three
themed walks: *Government and Democracy, Royal London* and
Upstairs, Downstairs. Led by a Tourist Board Official Guide and
run throughout the year. ***Meeting place***: the Tourist Information
Centre, Victoria Station Forecourt SW1 (**7 B2**). Charge.

Coach tours

Cityrama
Silverthorne Rd SW8. 071-720 6663. 20-mile sightseeing tour
of all the main London sights. Coaches leave *every 30 mins*
and takes *1-1½hrs*. Coaches leave from Trafalgar Square WC2
(**4 F4**), Westminster Abbey SW1 (**4 F6**), Piccadilly W1 (**4 C4**)
and Grosvenor Gdns SW1 (**7 B1**).

Evan Evans   4 E4
27 Cockspur St SW1. 071-930 2377. Well-established tour
company which operates a variety of tours; *full day, morning*
or *afternoon* plus a *2½hr* general drive around the capital and a
30-min cruise on the Thames.

Harrods   3 G6
Sightseeing Tours Dept, 4th Floor, Harrods, Knightsbridge
SW1. 071-730 1234. The most luxurious coach tour of
London, takes *2 hrs* with a taped commentary in several
languages and refreshments on board.

London Transport Sightseeing Tours
London Coaches, Jew's Row SW18. 081-877 1722. Round
London tours in traditional double-decker buses, some of
which are open-topped. A great favourite with children. *Phone
for further details.*

River trips and tours

*One of the best ways to appreciate London is to take a boat
trip. The Thames is a fascinatingly beautiful river, particularly
as it passes through the city, where the buildings lining its*

banks conjure up a whole host of historic, artistic and literary associations. Apart from the commuter Riverbus (see p23), there are several companies running river and canal trips. Daily river services run from the piers listed below, but you may board at any of the other piers en route.

NB: always check times of return boats at the pier on arrival.

DOWNRIVER SERVICES
Charing Cross Pier   4 F4
Victoria Embankment WC2. 071-839 3572. Trips to the Tower (20 mins) and Greenwich (45 mins) Apr-Oct every 30 mins between 10.30-16.00 Mon-Sun; Nov-Mar every 45 mins between 10.30-15.00 Mon-Sun.
Greenwich Pier
Return services to Charing Cross Pier (45 mins), Tower Pier (30 mins) and Westminster Pier (45 mins). Phone the individual pier for details.
Tower Pier   5 F4
071-488 0344. Trips to Greenwich (30 mins) every 30 mins 11.00-17.00 (16.00 winter) Mon-Sun, to Westminster (20 mins) every 20 mins 11.00-18.00 (17.00 winter) Mon-Sun. Ferry to HMS Belfast (5 mins) every 20 mins when Belfast is open (11.00-18.00 Mon-Sun, Sat & Sun only in winter). Ferry service enquiries: 071-407 6434.
Westminster Pier   4 F5
Victoria Embankment WC2. 071-930 4097. Trips to the Tower (25 mins) and Greenwich (45-50 mins) every 20 mins between 10.30-17.00 Mon-Sun. Special trips to the Thames Flood Barrier (75 mins each way) 10.00, 11.15, 13.30, 14.45. Luncheon cruises May-Oct 12.15-14.45 Wed & Sat, & Sun all year. Floodlit supper cruises May-Oct 20.30-22.30 Sun-Fri. Disco cruises 20.00-24.00 Fri & Sat all year.

UPRIVER SERVICES
These run from Westminster Pier only with all services calling at Putney Embankment.
Westminster Pier   4 F5
Victoria Embankment SW1. 071-930 4721. Trips to Putney (30 mins), Kew (90 mins), Richmond (2 hrs), Hampton Court (3-4 hrs).
From **Kew** boats leave Apr-Oct 10.30, 11.15, 12.00 then at 14.00, 14.45, 15.30 Mon-Sun.
From **Richmond** boats leave Apr-Oct 10.00, 10.30, 11.15, 12.00 Mon-Sun.
From **Hampton Court** boats leave Apr-Oct 10.00, 10.30, 11.15, 12.00 Mon-Sun. There are also local services to Hampton Court (Easter-mid Sep) from Richmond and Kingston. Phone 081-546 2434 for details.

UPPER THAMES
Salter Bros
Follybridge, Oxford. (0865) 243421. Salter's steamers run *May-Sep Mon-Sun.* Trips available from Oxford-Abingdon, Reading-Henley, Marlow-Windsor, Windsor-Staines.

Canal trips

Canal Waterbus   3 D1
cnr Westbourne Terrace & Warwick Crescent, Little Venice W9. 071-482 2550. Boats leave from Little Venice, stopping at London Zoo and continuing to Camden Lock. Round trip takes *1hr 50 mins. Apr-Sep 10.00-17.00 (on the hour) Mon-Sun; Oct-Mar 10.30, 12.00, 13.30 & 15.00 Sat & Sun.*

Jason's Trip   3 C1
opposite 60 Blomfield Rd W9. 071-286 3428. The traditional narrowboat *Jason* goes from Little Venice through Regent's Park and via London Zoo to Camden Lock, where you can disembark to explore Camden Market. Commentary and refreshments on board. Round trip takes *1 hr 30 mins. Easter-Oct 10.30, 12.30, 14.30 & 16.30 Mon-Sun. Nov-Feb private hire only.*

Jenny Wren Cruises   1 E1
250 Camden High St NW1. 071-485 4433. *Jenny Wren*, a traditional canal boat, goes from Camden Lock to Little Venice without stopping. The round trip takes *1 hr 30 mins. Mar-Oct 10.00, 11.30 & 14.00 Mon-Fri, 14.00 & 15.30 Sat, 11.30, 14.00 & 15.30 Sun. Nov-Feb private hire only.* Also run *My Fair Lady*, a cruising evening restaurant *19.30-23.00 Tue-Sat* and *Sun* lunchtime cruises *12.30-15.30.*

Zoos, safari parks and fun days out

Bekonscot Model Village
Warwick Rd, Beaconsfield, Bucks. (0494) 672919. 23 miles/37km west (A40, M40). Miniature wonderland set in the 1930s, created by Roland Callingham. Model railway travels around the village. It's surprising what you can discover if you take your time and look carefully. *Open Mar-Oct 10.00-17.00 Mon-Sun. Closed Nov-Feb.* Charge.

Chessington World of Adventures
Leatherhead Rd, Chessington, Surrey. (0372) 727227. 12 miles/19km south (A3, A243). 65 acres (27ha) comprising a zoo and theme park with wild rides such as Calamity Canyon and The Vampire – Britain's first hanging roller coaster. Also a bird garden, animal enclosure – where tame animals can be stroked – and a polar bear plunge. All attractions *open Apr-Oct*

10.00-17.00 Mon-Sun; zoo only *open Nov-Mar 10.00-16.00 Mon-Sun*. Charge.

Cotswold Wildlife Park

Burford, Oxon. (099382) 3006. 75 miles/120km west (M40, A40). Here it's the animals who roam in relative freedom in the 180 acres (75ha) and the public must keep to the carefully controlled walks. Zebras, rhino, deer, wallabies, antelope – they may well come and 'inspect' you! More dangerous species, such as leopards, are caged. Adventure playground and farmyard where tame animals can be stroked. Pony rides. Narrow gauge railway. Restaurant. Brass rubbing centre. *Open 10.00-18.00 (or dusk) Mon-Sun*. Charge.

London Zoo   1 C3

Regent's Park NW1. 071-722 3333. Famous zoo (under threat of closure at time of publication) with over 8000 residents. Aviary designed by Lord Snowdon. 'Moonlight World' reverses day and night so that rarely-seen nocturnal animals are kept awake during the day. *Open Mar-Oct 09.00-18.00 Mon-Sun (to 19.00 Bank hols & Sun preceding); Nov-Feb 10.00-16.00 Mon-Sun. Closed Xmas Day*. Charge.

Thorpe Park

Staines Rd, Chertsey, Surrey. (0932) 562633. 21 miles/34km south west (A308). A wonderful place for all ages, with lots of rides and entertainments such as Space Station Zero and Thunder River. Thorpe Farm is good for small children. All rides covered by entrance fee. *Open end Mar-end Oct 10.00-17.00 (to 18.00 Jul-Sep) Mon-Sun (last admission 2 hrs before closing time). Closed Nov-end Mar*. Charge (children under 3ft (1m) tall – free).

Whipsnade Wild Animal Park

Dunstable, Beds. (0582) 872171. 32 miles/51km north (M1, A5). Natural zoo of woods and downland with over 20,000 animals in large open-air enclosures. Some species roam freely. Travel round the park by car or the miniature motor coach train. *Open Apr-Oct 10.00-dusk Mon-Sun; Nov-Mar 10.00-16.00 Mon-Sun*. Charge.

Windsor Safari Park

Winkfield Rd, Windsor, Berks. (0753) 869841. 25 miles/40km west (M4). Drive round the park in your own car (nb: long queues in *summer*), to see a wide variety of wild animals. It is advisable to keep the windows closed and forbidden to get out of the car. Tropical plant and butterfly house, chimpanzee enclosure, dolphin, sealion and parrot shows. Also rides and entertainments. *Open 10.00-dusk (or 18.00) – (last admission 16.30) Mon-Sun*. Charge.

Woburn Wild Animal Kingdom & Leisure Park

Woburn, Beds. (0525 290407. 40 miles/64km north (M1).

Britain's largest drive-through safari park. Rare European bison, wallabies, llamas, rheas and other animals roam freely. Sealion and parrot shows. Leisure area with rides, boating lakes and cable car. 3000-acre (1250ha) park surrounding Woburn Abbey contains original herd of Père David deer. *Open mid Mar-end Oct 10.00-17.00 Mon-Sun. Closed Nov-mid Mar.* Charge.

Stately homes

Arundel Castle
Arundel, W. Sussex. (0903) 883136. 58 miles/93km south (A24, A29). Once an imposing feudal stronghold overlooking the River Arun. Home to the Dukes of Norfolk for 700 years. Magnificent collection of paintings by van Dyck, Holbein and Gainsborough. *Open Apr, May, Sep & Oct 13.00-17.00 Sun-Fri; Jun, Jul & Aug 12.00-17.00 Sun-Fri. Closed Nov-end Mar & all Bank hols. Last admission 1 hr before closing time.* Charge.

Blenheim Palace
Woodstock, Oxon. (0993) 811325. 60 miles/96km west (M40, A34). Birthplace of Sir Winston Churchill. Huge palace built 1705-22 by Sir John Vanbrugh. Fine example of English baroque architecture. Now home to the 11th Duke of Marlborough. Fine tapestries, sculpture and furnishings. *Open mid Mar-end Oct 10.30-17.30 Mon-Sun. Closed Nov-mid Mar.* Charge.

Goodwood
nr Chichester, W. Sussex. (0243) 774107. 60 miles/96km south (A3, A283, then A285 or A286). 18thC house by James Wyatt. Home to the 10th Duke of Richmond. Superb artistic connections, with masterpieces by Canaletto, van Dyck, Kneller and Reynolds. Also fine examples of French furniture, Sèvres porcelain and Gobelins tapestries. House often used for entertainment functions. Aerodrome and famous motor circuit nearby. Also its own race-course, where 'Glorious Goodwood', a famous meet, takes place at the *end Jul*. Advisable to phone in advance as there is *no public access on event days. Open May-end Sep 14.00-17.00 Sun & Mon (plus in Aug 14.00-17.00 Tue-Thur), Easter Sun & Mon. Closed on event days.* Charge.

Hatfield House
Hatfield, Herts. (0707) 262823. 21 miles/34km north (A1, A1000). Jacobean mansion built 1611 for Robert Cecil, 1st Earl of Salisbury. Still home to the Cecil family. Famous portraits, rare tapestries, fine furniture and armour. Tudor Old Royal Palace in grounds, where Queen Elizabeth I learned of her accession to the throne. Beautiful grounds with woodlands and lake. *Open (guided tours only) end Mar-Oct 12.00-17.00 Tue-Sat, 13.30-17.00 Sun. Closed Mon, except Bank hols 11.00-17.00 (no guided tours). Closed Nov-Mar.* Charge.

Leeds Castle
Maidstone, Kent. (0622) 765400. 40 miles/64km south east
(A20, M20). Beautiful, romantic, restored castle (AD 857).
Magnificent collection of medieval furnishings, French and
English fabrics, tapestries and paintings by Degas, Pissarro
and Vuillard. Delightful gardens. Shop, café, garden centre.
*Open Mar-Oct 11.00-18.00 Mon-Sun; Nov-Feb 11.00-17.00 Sat
& Sun (last admission 1 hr before closing time).* Charge.

Royal Pavilion, Brighton
Old Steine, Brighton, E. Sussex. (0273) 603005. 45
miles/72km south (A23). Fantastic Oriental seaside 'villa' with
onion domes and minarets built for the Prince Regent (later
George IV) by Nash 1815-22. Lavish Chinese-style staterooms.
*Open Jun-Sep 10.00-18.00 Mon-Sun; Oct-May 10.00-17.00
Mon-Sun.* Charge.

Windsor Castle
Windsor, Berks. (0753) 868286. 20 miles/32km west (M4).
Imposing 800-year-old medieval fortress. 12thC Round Tower
built by Henry II; St George's Chapel fine example of 16thC
perpendicular. Magnificent State Apartments. Still used by
present Royal Family so opening times are complex. Castle
precinct *open Mar & Apr, Sep & Oct 10.00-17.15 Mon-Sun;
May-Aug 10.00-19.15 Mon-Sun; Nov-Mar 10.00-16.15 Mon-
Sun. Closed Garter Day (2nd or 3rd Mon in Jun) and any State
Visit arrival day.* Charge. State Apartments *open May-Oct
10.30-17.00 Mon-Sat, 13.30-17.00 Sun; Nov-Apr 10.30-15.00
Mon-Sat. Closed Sun. Closed when Queen is in residence –
usually 6 weeks at Easter, 3 weeks in Jun and 3 weeks at
Xmas.* Charge.

Woburn Abbey
Woburn, Beds. (0525) 290666. 40 miles/64km north (M1).
Home of Dukes of Bedford for over 300 years. Built on the
site of a Cistercian monastery, founded 1145. Present building
dates from 17thC and 18thC. Set in 3000-acre park, part of
which is now a safari park (see p70). Collection of paintings
includes works by Rembrandt, Gainsborough, Holbein and
Canaletto. *Open Jan-Mar 11.00-16.00 Mon-Sun; Apr-Oct
11.00-17.00 Mon-Sat, 11.00-17.30 Sun & Bank hols. Closed
Nov-Dec.* Charge.

Day trips

*The telephone numbers listed in the following entries refer to
the Tourist Information centre in the town.*

Bath
107 miles/171km west (M4, A4). ⇌: Paddington. (0225)
462831. Elegant Georgian town, rich in architectural detail.

See the dramatic sweeping curve of Ionic columns forming the Royal Crescent. Several museums including Roman Baths with natural hot springs, from which the town got its name and indeed its existence. Good shops.

Brighton

56 miles/90km south (A23). ⇌: Victoria. (0273) 23755. Originally a poor fishing village which became fashionable when the Royal Pavilion was built here (see p72). Splendid Regency terraces, five miles of beach and interesting shops in The Lanes; unusual jewellery, antiques, clothes and artefacts. The Victorian pier (recently restored) has plenty of attractions for the family. Newly developed marina has waterside pubs and cafés.

Cambridge

60 miles/96km north (M11). ⇌: King's Cross. (0223) 322640. University city of spires, mellow colleges and riverside meadows, bordering the River Cam. Hire a punt to view the university colleges and serene lawns. 31 colleges in total, the oldest, Peterhouse, was established in 1284. King's College Chapel is one of the world's Gothic masterpieces. The Fitzwilliam Museum has a superb collection of classical antiquities and paintings.

Henley-on-Thames

Oxon. 36 miles/57km west (A4). ⇌: Paddington. (0993) 778800. Situated on a very pretty part of the Thames and most famous for the Regatta, held in *early Jul* (see p50). Arched bridge was built in 1786. In St Mary's churchyard are 16thC almshouses and a rare unspoilt 15thC timber-framed building – the Chantry House. The Regatta is held on the straight mile of river downstream from the bridge.

Oxford

56 miles/90km west (M40). ⇌: Paddington. (0865) 726871. A University city of 'dreaming spires' and fine college buildings. 30 colleges, all worth a visit – the grandest being Christ Church and the oldest University College (1249). Other attractions include the Sheldonian Theatre by Wren, the 15thC Bodleian Library, the Ashmolean Museum, and the oldest botanic gardens in Britain. In addition there are several good pubs and restaurants.

Stratford-on-Avon

Warks. 90 miles/144km north west (M40, A34). ⇌: Liverpool Street. (0789) 293127. The birthplace of William Shakespeare (1564-1616). The town is still Elizabethan in atmosphere, with overhanging gables and timbered inns. Visit the writer's birthplace in Henley Street, his house at New Place, Anne Hathaway's cottage and the museum and picture gallery. The Shakespeare Memorial Theatre in Waterside is thriving and progressive.

SHOPPING

Generally shops open 09.00/10.00-17.30/18.00 Mon-Sat and are closed on Sun & Bank hols. *Many Bond Street shops* do not open on Sat. *In cases where a shop's hours differ from the standard times above, the opening hours appear in* italic *at the end of the entry. Some areas have a late shopping night. See individual shopping areas below.*

Tax free shopping

Most goods and services in the UK are subject to VAT (value added tax) at the standard rate of 17½%. Luxury items – such as tobacco, perfume, alcoholic beverages and motor vehicles – are subject to higher rates. A good way to purchase tax-free goods is to shop in stores showing the London Tax Free Shopping sign. This system entails filling in a voucher, presenting it to customs with the goods and returning it to the London Tax Free Shopping organisation which will then immediately refund your money in the currency of your country of residence.

Shopping areas

Camden   1 D2
A popular and trendy canalside area lined with shops and a huge, sprawling market. Come here if you're looking for period clothes, alternative books, imported records, pine furniture and artefacts. It's at its busiest and liveliest on *Sat & Sun afternoons.*

Covent Garden   4 F3
Once the site of the famous fruit and vegetable market, this refurbished area is now a fashionable pedestrianised piazza. The arcades are lined with small specialist fashion and gift shops, plus plenty of places to eat and drink. There are also open-air craft stalls, an antiques market and an occasional craft market. Leading off the piazza in every direction, the streets reveal an interesting variety of shops and restaurants with the latest in fashion, high-tech household equipment and exotic foods. *Late night Thur.*

Kensington High Street   3 B6
Less hectic than Oxford Street, though a similar range of shops and large branches of most high street chains, plus

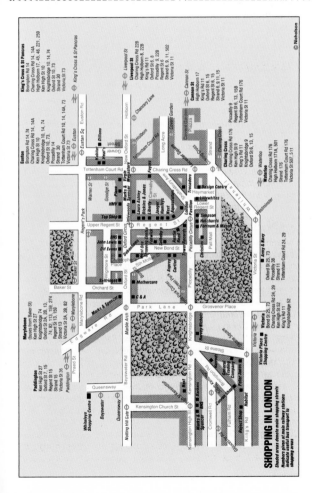

SHOPS

Aquascutum 734 6090
Army & Navy 834 1234
Asprey 493 6767
Austin Reed 734 6789
BHS (Kensington High St) 937 0919
BHS (Oxford St) 629 2011
Barkers 937 5432
C & A 629 7272
Cartier 493 6962
Christies 839 9060
Conran Shop 589 7401
DH Evans 629 8800
Debenhams 580 3000
Design Centre 839 8000
Dickins & Jones 734 7070
Dillons 636 1577
Fenwick 629 9161
Fortnum & Mason 734 8040
Foyles 437 5660
General Trading Company 730 0411
Habitat (King's Rd) 351 1211
Habitat (Tottenham Court Rd) 631 3880
Hamleys 734 3161
Harrods 730 1234
Harvey Nichols 235 5000
Hatchards 439 9921
Heal's 636 1666
HMV 631 3423
Jaeger 734 8211
John Lewis 629 7711
Laura Ashley (Regent St) 437 9760
Liberty 734 1234
Lillywhites 930 3181
Littlewoods 434 4301
London Pavilion 437 1838
Marks & Spencer (Ken. High St) 938 3711
Marks & Spencer (Marble Arch) 935 7954
Marks & Spencer (Oxford St) 437 7722
Mothercare 629 6621
Next (Kensington High St) 938 4211
Next (Regent St) 434 2515
Peter Jones 730 3434
Plaza on Oxford St) 637 8811
Reject Shop 352 2750
Selfridges 629 1234
Simpson 734 2002
Sotheby's 493 8080
Top Shop 636 7700
Tower Records 439 2500
Trocadero 439 1791
Victoria Place Shopping Centre 931 8811
Virgin Megastore 631 1234

SHOPPING IN LONDON

Shaded areas denote main shopping streets

Numbers given at main railway stations indicate useful bus transport to shopping areas

© Nicholson

Barkers of Kensington, its own department store. Delve into the roads leading off for more individual (and more expensive) fashion shops. *Late night Thur.*

King's Road/Chelsea 6 E3

Still as much a place to be seen in as to see, this area really comes alive on *Sat* with the parading trendies outdoing each other in outrageousness. One of the centres for up-to-the-minute fashion, plus high street chains, it is particularly good for shoes and men's clothing. *Late night Wed.*

Knightsbridge 3 G5

A traditionally fashionable area for the rich and famous, dominated by Harrods and Harvey Nichols. Beauchamp Place also has exclusive furniture, jewellery and clothes. *Late night Wed.*

Piccadilly/Trocadero/London Pavilion 4 E3

Quality and tradition in the form of Fortnum & Mason, Hatchards, Simpson, and Lillywhites. Also the historic Burlington Arcade. The Trocadero and London Pavilion cater for the more up-to-date taste with one-stop shopping, refreshment and entertainment, while Tower Records dominates Piccadilly Circus from the old Swan & Edgar building. *Many shops open late Mon-Sat.*

Soho 4 E2

Much less sleazy, but as cosmopolitan as ever, Soho is an excellent location for specialist shopping. International food shops, oriental supermarkets, and designer clothes. Also trendy restaurants and wine bars. Berwick Street Market and Chinatown both merit a visit.

West End

London's biggest shopping area consisting of three main streets. **Oxford Street (4 C2)** is over a mile long and has nearly all the major department stores including Selfridges, John Lewis, London's largest Marks & Spencer and an overwhelming assortment of individual fashion shops. It gets very crowded here, especially on *Sat* and at *lunchtime*. **Regent Street (4 D3)** is less hectic and offers luxurious items and gifts at Liberty, plus several china, glass and clothing stores and the department store Dickins & Jones. **Carnaby Street (4 D3)** is still worth a visit. World-renowned in the 1960s, it has retained its busy and lively atmosphere, with frequent pavement shows and interesting clothes and souvenir shops. Some of the high street chains have now also moved in. For real luxury try **New Bond Street (4 C3)** where you'll find shoes, jewellery, prints, pictures and designer clothes. Two pedestrianised streets just off Oxford Street, and well worth exploring, are **St Christopher's Place (4 B2)** and **South Molton Street (4 C2)**. Both are packed with stylish small shops and attractive eating places. *Late night Thur.*

Whiteleys 3 C3

Queensway W2. One of the first department stores, now transformed into a smart, cosmopolitan complex of shops, cafés, restaurants, bars and an eight-screen cinema. *Many shops open late Mon-Sat.*

Department stores

Army & Navy 7 C1

101-105 Victoria St SW1. 071-834 1234. Excellent food hall and wine department. Clothing, cosmetics, household goods, toys, books, china and glass. Hairdressing salon. Coffee shop. Restaurant. *Open 09.30-18.00 Mon-Sat (to 19.00 Thur).*

Barkers of Kensington 3 C5

63 Kensington High St W8. 071-937 5432. Fashionable clothes, household and electrical goods and a hairdressing/beauty salon. Restaurant. Café. *Open 09.30-18.00 Mon-Fri (to 20.00 Thur), 09.30-18.30 Sat.*

BHS (British Home Stores) 4 C2

252 Oxford St W1. 071-629 2011. Inexpensive clothes and accessories for men, women and children. Household goods and extensive lighting department. Restaurant. *Open 09.00-18.00 Mon, Tue & Sat, to 19.00 Wed & Fri, to 20.00 Thur.*

Debenhams 4 D2

344-348 Oxford St W1. 071-580 3000. Fashion clothes at reasonable prices. Good departments for kitchenware, lingerie, hosiery and cosmetics. Restaurant. *Open 09.00-18.00 Mon, 10.00-18.00 Tue, 09.30-19.00 Wed-Fri, 09.30-18.30 Sat.*

Dickins & Jones 4 D3

224 Regent St W1. 071-734 7070. Fashionable store selling stylish ladies' and men's clothes, accessories and haberdashery. Excellent and wide range of dress fabrics. Also china and glass departments. Hairdressers. Beauty salon. Restaurant. Coffee shop. *Open 09.30-18.00 Mon-Sat (to 20.00 Thur).*

D.H. Evans 4 D2

318 Oxford St W1. 071-629 8800. Part of the House of Fraser group with excellent fashion and lingerie departments. Unusual sizes are well catered for in the dress department. Also perfumery, furniture and household goods. Astral Sports is in the basement. Restaurant. Café. *Open 09.30-18.00 Mon-Fri (to 20.00 Thur), 09.00-19.00 Sat.*

Fenwicks 4 C3

63 New Bond St W1. 071-629 9161. Good fashions and accessories. Imaginative gifts and stationery and a wide selection of books. *Open 09.00-18.00 Mon-Sat (to 19.30 Thur).*

Fortnum & Mason 4 D4

181 Piccadilly W1. 071-734 8040. Well-established and

respected store. Famous for its exotic foods, but also offers jewellery, china, glass, fashion, perfumery, leather goods, toys, stationery and a beauty salon. Two restaurants. Tea room. *Open 09.00-17.30 Mon-Fri, to 17.00 Sat.*

Harrods   3 G6
Knightsbridge SW1. 071-730 1234. The world's most famous department store – over 60 fashion departments with men's, ladies' and children's clothing and accessories. Also perfumes, gifts, china, glass, pets, toys, books, furniture and fabrics. The Edwardian marble food halls are well worth a visit for their luxury foods. Wide range of services. Bureau de change. Barber's shop. Hairdressers. Beauty salon. Six restaurants. Three coffee shops. *Open 09.00-18.00 Mon-Sat (to 20.00 Wed).*

Harvey Nichols   4 A5
Knightsbridge SW1. 071-235 5000. Elegant, stylish clothes from top British, Continental and American designers. Home furnishings and household goods. Restaurant. *Open 10.00-19.00 Mon-Fri, to 18.00 Sat.*

Heal's/Habitat   4 E1
196 Tottenham Court Rd W1. 071-631 3880. Terence Conran's brainchild – Habitat offers affordable furniture, kitchenware, rugs, stationery, posters. Heal's is more expensive with more unusual designs and gift ideas. Restaurant. *Open 09.30-18.00 Mon-Sat (to 19.30 Thur).*

John Lewis   4 C2
278-306 Oxford St W1. 071-629 7711. One of the largest dress fabric departments in Europe, as well as furniture, furnishings, china, glass, household goods and fashions. Excellent haberdashery department. Bureau de change. Interpreters available. NB: they do not take credit cards. Restaurant. Coffee shop. Other branches. *Open 09.00-17.30 Mon-Sat (09.30-20.00 Thur).*

Liberty   4 D3
210-220 Regent St W1. 071-734 1234. Famous and fashionable, well-known for distinctive fabrics and unusual luxury goods. Good selection of unusual jewellery and rare gifts, plus glass, china, oriental rugs, prints, gifts and several designer-label collections. Restaurant. Coffee shop. *Open 09.30-18.00 Mon-Sat (to 19.30 Thur).*

Littlewoods   4 B2
508-520 Oxford St W1. 071-629 7840. Inexpensive high-street chain for clothing and household goods. *Open 09.00-19.00 Mon-Sat (to 20.00 Thur).*

Marks & Spencer   4 B2
458 Oxford St W1. 071-935 7954. Well-loved chain with good quality inexpensive clothing and accessories for men, women and children. Wide range of foods, home furnishings, cosmetics

and gifts. Other branches. Bureau de change. NB: they do not take credit cards. *Open 09.00-19.00 Mon-Wed, to 20.00 Thur & Fri, to 18.30 Sat.*

Peter Jones   **6 F2**
Sloane Sq SW1. 071-730 3434. (Part of same chain as John Lewis). Excellent quality and good value clothing, accessories and household goods. Also modern and antique furniture, glass, china, and a large furnishing fabric department. Interpreters available. Restaurant. Coffee shop. NB: they do not take credit cards. *Open 09.00-17.30 Mon-Sat (09.30-19.00 Wed).*

Selfridges   **4 B2**
400 Oxford St W1. 071-629 1234. Vast store with huge range of clothing, accessories and household goods. Also toys, sports clothing and equipment and an impressive food hall. Three restaurants. Five cafés. *Open 09.30-18.00 Mon-Fri (to 20.00 Thur), 09.00-18.00 Sat.*

Clothes stores

Nearly all London's department stores also have extensive collections of clothes and accessories. These are the specialists:

Aquascutum   **4 D3**
100 Regent St W1. 071-734 6090. Fine quality British raincoats, coats, suits, knitwear and accessories for men and women.

Austin Reed   **4 D3**
103 Regent St W1. 071-734 6789. English and Continental suits and accessories for men. Accent on quality. Valet service and barber. Also ladies' clothing, executive suits, designer wear and classic dresses.

Burberrys   **4 E3**
18 Haymarket SW1. 071-930 3343. Classic raincoats for men and women cut in the English style. Hats, scarves, suits and accessories. Other branches.

C&A   **4 B2**
501-509 Oxford St W1. 071-629 7272. Vast selection of reasonably priced fashions and classics for all the family including skirts, dresses, coats, knitwear, suits and leathers. Clockhouse is for 14-25 year-olds. Good selection of sports clothing, especially ski wear. Other branches. *Open 09.30-19.00 Mon-Fri (to 20.00 Thur), 09.00-18.00 Sat.*

Jaeger   **4 D3**
200-206 Regent St W1. 071-734 8211. Four floors of well-cut, fashionable English clothes. Suits, coats, knitwear and casual wear for men; dresses, suits and separates for women in colour co-ordinated departments. Accessories, jewellery, perfumes and Italian footwear. Other branches.

Conversion charts

Clothing Sizes
In London you will find English, Continental and American sizing in clothes shops, whereas there is a combination of English and Continental sizing for shoes.

Dresses

English	10	12	14	16	18	20	22
	32	**34**	**36**	**38**	**40**	**42**	**44**
USA	8	10	12	14	16	18	20
Continental	38	40	42	44	46	48	50

Shoes

English	3	$3\frac{1}{2}$	4	$4\frac{1}{2}$	5	$5\frac{1}{2}$	6	$6\frac{1}{2}$	7	$7\frac{1}{2}$	8
USA	$4\frac{1}{2}$	5	$5\frac{1}{2}$	6	$6\frac{1}{2}$	7	$7\frac{1}{2}$	8	$8\frac{1}{2}$	9	$9\frac{1}{2}$
Continental	35	36	37	37	38	38	39	40	40	41	41

Hats

English	$6\frac{5}{8}$	$6\frac{3}{4}$	$6\frac{7}{8}$	7	$7\frac{1}{8}$	$7\frac{1}{4}$	$7\frac{3}{8}$	$7\frac{1}{2}$	$7\frac{5}{8}$
USA	$6\frac{3}{4}$	$6\frac{7}{8}$	7	$7\frac{1}{8}$	$7\frac{3}{8}$	$7\frac{1}{2}$			
Continental	54	55	56	57	58	59	60	61	62

Glove sizes are international.

Weights and Measures

Feet/Metres

English	1	2	3	4	5	6	7	8	9	10
Continental	0.3	0.6	0.9	1.2	1.5	1.8	2.1	2.4	2.7	3.0

Pounds/Kilograms

English	1	2	3	4	5	6	7	8	9	10
Continental	0.4	0.9	1.4	1.8	2.3	2.7	3.2	3.6	4.1	4.5

Pints/Litres

English	$\frac{1}{4}$	$\frac{1}{2}$	$\frac{3}{4}$	1	2	3	4	5
Continental	0.1	0.3	0.4	0.6	1.1	1.7	2.3	2.8

Lillywhites 4 E3
Piccadilly Circus W1. 071-930 3181. Five floors of sports clothing and equipment for just about any sport you can think of.

Moss Bros 4 F3
27-29 King St WC2. 071-240 4567. Men's ceremonial and formal wear. Morning suits, dinner jackets, bow ties, top hat and tails, accessories. Arrange hire at least one week in advance. Deposit required. Other branches.

Next & Next Man 4 C2
325 Oxford St W1. 071-491 4059. Fashions for men, women and children. Also cosmetics, lingerie, accessories, flowers and home furnishings. Other branches.

Simpson 4 D4
203 Piccadilly W1. 071-734 2002. High-quality clothing for men and women. Shirts, knitwear, dresses and separates. Daks country clothes, luggage and accessories. Restaurant.

Antiques

Good hunting grounds are the King's Road, Portobello Road, Camden Passage in Islington, Kensington Church Street, Fulham Road and Camden Town.

Antiquarius 6 E3
135-141 King's Rd SW3. 071-352 7989. Over 150 stalls with clothing, jewellery, china, glass, books and prints.

Chelsea Antiques Market 6 E4
245-253 King's Rd SW3. 071-352 9695. Large, busy market – period clothing, watches, books, clocks, prints and scientific instruments.

Gallery of Antique Costume & Textiles
2 Church St NW8. 071-723 9981. Suppliers of antique costumes and textiles including clothing and fabrics from all over the world. Reasonable prices.

Grays Antiques Market 4 C3
1-7 Davies Mews W1. 071-629 7034. Two huge Victorian warehouses with wide selection of antiques – luggage, leather goods, toys, games and jewellery.

Auctioneers

W.& F.C. Bonham & Sons 3 F6
Montpelier Galleries, Montpelier St SW7. 071-584 9161. Paintings, furniture, carpets, porcelain, jewellery and silver. Branch: 65-69 Lots Rd SW10. 071-351 7111.

Christie's 4 D4
8 King St SW1. 071-839 9060. Internationally famous. Comprehensive fine art auctioneers since 1766. Free estimates. Branch: 85 Old Brompton Rd SW7. 071-581 7611.

Sotheby's   **4 C3**
34-35 New Bond St W1. 071-493 8080. Internationally famous for antiques and works of art. Paintings, ceramics, glass, furniture, silver, jewellery, books and manuscripts.

Books

Dillons   **1 F6**
82 Gower St W1. 071-636 1577. Vast stock of paperbacks and hardbacks with large academic range including scientific and language books. Other branches. *Open 09.30-22.00 Mon-Sat, 11.00-19.30 Sun.*

Foyles   **4 E2**
119-125 Charing Cross Rd WC2. 071-437 5660. London's largest book store with practically every English book in print.

Hatchards   **4 D4**
187 Piccadilly W1. 071-439 9921. Something of an institution with a comprehensive selection of general books and knowledgeable staff.

W.H. Smith   **6 F2**
36 Sloane Sq SW1. 071-730 0351. Well-known retailer, with a wide choice of books, magazines, stationery, records, tapes, CDs and games. Many other branches.

Waterstones   **3 C5**
193 Kensington High St W8. 071-8432. Excellent general store with comprehensive selections in just about every subject you can think of. *Open 09.30-22.00 Mon-Fri, to 19.00 Sat, 11.00-18.00 Sun.*

Crafts

Contemporary Applied Arts   **4 F2**
43 Earlham St WC2. 071-836 6993. Comprehensive display of work by craftsmen using a variety of materials. Many British pieces.

Naturally British   **4 F3**
13 New Row WC2. 071-240 0551. High-quality hand-made British goods including pottery, toys, gifts, clothes, hand-knits and jewellery.

Food

Fortnum & Mason, Harrods and Selfridges have particularly impressive food halls. The following are more specialist shops:

H.R. Higgins   **4 D4**
79 Duke St W1. 071-629 3913. Over 40 types of coffee including original and blended, light, medium and dark roasts.

Hobbs & Co   **4 B3**
29 South Audley St W1. 071-409 1058. Gourmet food and

drink: cheeses, pâtés, wines, pâtisserie, preserves and condiments, fruit and vegetables.

Paxton & Whitfield 4 D4

93 Jermyn St W1. 071-930 0259. Over 250 superb English and Continental cheeses plus traditional hams, home-made pies and pâtés.

Gifts

Covent Garden General Store 4 F3

111 Long Acre WC2. 071-240 0331. Well-established shop selling a huge range of tasteful gifts including pottery, comestibles, caneware and ornaments. *Open 10.00-23.00 Mon-Wed, to 24.00 Thur-Sat, 11.00-21.00 Sun.*

Crabtree & Evelyn 3 B4

6 Kensington Church St W8. 071-937 9335. Exquisite perfumes and toiletries for men and women. All beautifully packaged. Other branches.

General Trading Company 6 F2

144 Sloane St SW1. 071-730 0411. Some of the best designs in contemporary English and Continental glass and china. Café.

Old Curiosity Shop 4 F3

13 Portsmouth St WC2. 071-405 9891. Immortalised by Dickens, the shop sells gifts, curios and antiques.

Markets

Berwick Street 4 E2

W1. Busy and boisterous general market in the heart of Soho. Good value fruit and vegetables, also meat, cheeses, fresh fish and household goods. *Open 09.00-18.00 Mon-Sat.*

Camden Lock 1 D1

Where Chalk Farm Rd crosses Regent's Canal NW1. Among the cobbled courtyards and warehouses of the lock is a huge market area selling everything from designer clothes and pine furniture to antique clothing and junk. Also interesting food stalls. *Open 08.00-18.00 Mon-Sat.*

Petticoat Lane 5 F1

The name given to the market radiating from Middlesex Street. Probably named after the second-hand clothes dealers who had their businesses here in the early 1600s. Lively and hectic, with mainly clothing on sale, but also toys, food, toiletries and luxury goods. *Open 09.00-14.00 Sun only.*

Portobello Road 3 A2

W11. Well-known and much-frequented – fruit, vegetables and new goods sold *09.00-18.00 Mon-Sat (to 13.00 Thur)*, second-hand junk and bric-à-brac sold *08.00-17.00 Fri*, and the famous antiques market is held *08.00-17.00 Sat.*

Oxford Street

Left side	No.	No.	Right side
Fashion M **Hornes**	4	7	**Coles** Fashion M
Pub **The Tottenham**	6		Tottenham Court Road
Restaurant **McDonald's**	8	15	**K Shoes** Shoes FM
Sock Shop	10	17	**Wigwam** Gifts
Mecca Entertainment & Catering	12	19	**Regent School of Languages**
Records **Virgin Megastore**	14	19	**Challoner** Employment agency
Cannon Cinema	18	19	**Claude Gill** Books
Comics & books **Virgin**	22	25	**Messrs C** Foods
Souvenirs **Cerex**	24	27	**Tandy** Electronics
Records **Virgin Megastore**	26	29	**Pizza Hut** Restaurant
Sotheby's Library & Educational Services	30	33	**Nick Nack** Gifts
Lloyds Bank	32	35	**Papagallo's** Take-away food
Shoes FM **Barratts**	36	37	**Ryman** Stationery
Fashion FM **Jeans West**	38	37	**Spats** Club
National Westminster Bank	40	41	**Cardshops** Cards & posters
Fashion & bags **Opened**	44	43	**Chequepoint** Bureau de change
Natural beauty products **Eternité**	46	45	**John Kent** Fashion M
Restaurant **Angus Steak House**	48	45	**Mayfair School of English**
		47	**Key** Employment agency
		47	**Sonico Jeans Centre** Fashion FM
		49a	**Outlet** Fashion M
		49	**Kelly** Employment agency
		51	**The Boot Store**
		53	**Pan Air** Travel
		53	**Mondo Pelle** Leather fashion
		55	**Suits You** Fashion M

Hanway Street   **Soho Street**

Left side	No.	No.	Right side
Jewellers **Gold Warehouse**	50	61	**Ratners** Jewellers
Midland Bank	52	63	**Chequepoint** Bureau de change
		65	**LIA Amusement Arcade**
		67	**CJ's** Gifts

Rathbone Place

Left side	No.	No.	Right side
Fashion FM **Ultimate Clothing Co**	54	73	**Mash** Fashion M
Fashion FM **Lace**	58	75	**Avirex USA** Fashion M
Building society **Halifax**	60	79	**79 Wine Bar**
Natural beauty products **The Body Shop**	66	83	**Exclusive Leather Wear** Fashion FM
Handbags **Salisburys**	68a	85	**Marmalade** Fashion F
Hi-fi **McDonalds**	70	87	**Pizza Hut** Restaurant
Gifts & cards **Oxford News**	78	89	**Sock Shop**
Computer games **Microbyte**	80		
Shoes FM **Dolcis**	82		
Cameras & electronics **Dixons**	86		

Dean Street

Left side	No.	No.	Right side
		91	**Tie Rack** Fashion M
		93	**Knickerbox** Underwear
		95	**Bureau de change**
		97	**Woodhouse** Fashion M
		101	**Cerex** Souvenirs

Newman Street   **Great Chapel Street**

Left side	No.	No.	Right side
Opticians **For Eyes**	92	103	**Slot Machine** Fashion FM
Chemist **Boots**	94	105	**Sendean** Camera repairs
Virgin Games Centre	100	107	**London Executive Briefcase Centre**
Nightclub **100 Club**	100	107	**Silverdale** Travel goods
Fashion F **Stirling Cooper**	104	109	**Mark-One** Fashion M
Fashion M **The Suit House**	110	111	**Cobra** Sports goods
National Westminster Bank	112	113	**Video Palace** Videos
		115	**Warrior** Fashion M
		117	**Athena** Posters, cards, gifts
		121	**Skin Image** Fashion F

Berners Street   **Wardour Street**

Left side	No.	No.	Right side
Fashion F **Principles**	114	127	**Instyle Clothing** Fashion M & gifts
Fashion M **High & Mighty**	116	129	**Bobtails** Hair Salon
Fashion M **Tie Rack**	118	129	**Video Clearance Store** Videos
SHOPPING CENTRE **THE PLAZA**		137	**Footsie 100** Shoes FM
Shoes FM **Pumps**	120	139	**Callan School of English**
Fashion M **Filmore**	122	141	**Rush Me** Fashion F
Fashion FM **The Gap**	124	143	**Baloughi** Souvenirs

Wells Street   **Berwick Street**

Left side	No.	No.	Right side
Sportswear **Olympus**	134	145	**J. D. Sports** Sportswear
Fashion M **Nickleby's**	136	145	**Accountants on Call**
Fashion M **Mister Byrite**	140	147	**Sacha/Red or Dead** Shoes FM
Restaurant **Burger King**	142	147	**Cornet** Travel
Novelties, cards **Cascade**	146	149	**Coles** Fashion M
Employment agency **Action Secretary**	146	151	**Workflow** Employment agency
Records **HMV**	150	151	**Boots** Chemist
Fashion M **Oakland**	156	153	**Jane Norman** Fashion F
Fashion M **Profile**	160	155	**The Sale** Fashion FM
Fashion M **Review**	162	159	**Shellys** Shoes

Poland Street

Left side	No.	No.	Right side
		163	**Books Etc** Books
		165	**Abbey National** Building society
		167	**H.Samuel** Jewellers
		173	**MARKS & SPENCER** STORE
		175	**Saxone** Shoes FM
		181	**Ecco** Temporary services
		181	**Next** Employment agency
		181	**Dolcis** Shoes FM
		185	**McDonald's** Restaurant
		189	**Next** Fashion FM

Winsley Street

Left side	No.	No.	Right side
Fashion M **Blazer**	170		
Sportswear **Champion**	172		
Fashion F **Richards**	174		
Baby store **Mothercare**	174		
Fashion FM **Merk-One**	178		

Great Titchfield Street   **Ramilles Street**

Left side	No.	No.	Right side
Shoes FM **Ravel**	184	199	**Leslie Davis** Jewellers
Sock Shop	190	201	**Paperchase** Gifts
Shoes FM **Faith**	192	213	**LITTLEWOODS** STORE
Restaurant **Burger Delight**	192	217	**Wallis** Fashion F
Midland Bank	196	219	**Ratners** Jewellers
STORE **C&A**	202		

Great Portland Street			**Hills Place**
Restaurant **Burger King**	214	221	**Miss Selfridge** Fashion F
Fashion M **Peter Brown**	220	225	**Benetton** Fashion FM
Fashion M **Burton**	222	227	**Splash** Souvenirs
		231	**Jeans West** Fashion FM
		233	**Mister Byrite** Fashion M
		235	Thomas Cook Bureau de change
Argyll Street			
STORE **TOP SHOP & TOP MAN**	214-216	241	Exchange International Bureau de change
		266	**Waterford/Wedgwood** China & glass
Oxford Circus			**Regent Street**
Fashion F **Hennes**	240	251	South African Airways
		257	**Sock Shop**
John Prince's Street		261	**For Eyes** Opticians
		263	**Richards** Fashion F
Fashion M **Mister Byrite**	244	267	**J. D. Sports** Sportswear
Shoes FM **Bally**	246	271	**Le Croissant** Take-away food
Shoes FM **Ravel**	248	273	**Scottish Woollens** Fashion, knitwear
Jewellers **H. Samuel**	250	275	Salvation Army Hall
STORE **BHS**	252	277	**Ernest Jones** Jewellers
Shoes FM **Clarks**	260	283	**River Island** Fashion FM
Fashion F **Jane Norman**	262	285	**Oddball Clothing Co** Fashion FM
Fashion FM **Dash**	266	287	**Cecil Gee** Fashion M
Natural beauty products **The Body Shop**	268	289	**The Deep Pan Pizza Co** Restaurant
Greetings cards **Clinton**	270	291	Bureau de change
Fashion F **Wallis**	272	291	**Mr Howard** Fashion M
		291	**Genel** Fashion FM
		293	**McDonald's** Restaurant
Holles Street			**Harewood Place**
STORE **JOHN LEWIS**	273-306	295	**Saxone** Shoes FM
		297	**Tie Rack** Fashion M
		299	**Babers** Shoes M
		299	Manpower Employment agency
		299	Noel Nursing agency
		301	**Olympus Sports** Sports wear
		303	**Burton** Fashion M
		309	**Dorothy Perkins** Fashion F
Old Cavendish Street		309	**Ratners** Jewellers
		315	Acme Employment agency
STORE **D.H. EVANS**	318	315	**The Gap** Fashion FM
Chapel Place			**Dering Street**
Shoes FM **K Shoes**	324	321	**Stefanel** Fashion F
Shoes FM **Sacha**	326	321	Berlitz School of Languages
Fashion FM **Benetton**	328	321	**Next** Fashion M
Smokers' materials **Bond's**	328	325	**Next** Fashion F
Bank of Scotland	332		
Vere Street			**New Bond Street**
STORE **DEBENHAMS**	344-348	333	**Dolcis** Shoes FM
		335	**Splash** Souvenirs
		337	**Bonjour Paris** Take-away food
		339	Bureau de change
		341	West End Travel
		341	Tea Board of India
Marylebone Lane			**Woodstock Street**
TSB Bank	350	351	**Le Croissant** Take-away food
Souvenirs **Cerex**	352	353	**Thorntons** Chocolates
Fashion FM **Oddball Clothing Co**	356	353	Brook Street Employment agency
National Westminster Bank	358	355	**Scottish Woollens** Fashion FM
		357	**Selection** Fashion FM
			Sedley Place
		359	**Churchill** Gifts
		361	**Oakland** Fashion M
		363	**HMV** Records
		369	**La Brioche Dorée** Take-away food
		369a	Foreign Exchange Corporation
			Bond Street
		373	**Leslie Davis** Jewellers
Stratford Place			**Davies Street (South Molton Street)**
Shoes FM **Lilley & Skinner**	360	379	WEST ONE SHOPPING CENTRE
Fashion F **Kookai**	362	383	**Faith** Shoes F
Fashion M **Woodhouse**	364	385	**Boots** Chemist
Jewellers **H. Samuel**	366	393	**Coles** Fashion M
		395	**The Gap** Fashion FM
St Christopher's Place			
Shoes FM **Bally**	368		
Fashion M **Suits You**	370		
Natural beauty products **The Body Shop**	372		
James Street			**Gilbert Street**
STORE **C&A**	376	399	**Pizzaland** Restaurant
		399	Lloyds Bank
Bird Street			**Binney Street**
Shoes FM **Instep Sports**	386	407	**David Clulow** Opticians
Fashion F **Jane Norman**	388	409	**Bertie** Shoes FM
Shoes FM **Barratts**	388	409	**Review** Fashion M
		411	Kelly Temporary services
		413	National Westminster Bank

Duke Street | | **Duke Street**

| | 415 | **Hornes** *Fashion M* |
| | 419 | **Principles** *Fashion FM* |

Lumley Street

| | 429 | **Burger King** *Restaurant* |

STORE **SELFRIDGES** 400 | | **Balderton Street**

	431	Midland Bank
	435	**Sock Shop**
	439	**Boots** *Chemist*
	443	British Nursing Association
	443	**Churchill** *Gifts*
	445	**London House** *Fashion FM*
	447	**Grip** *Fashion M*
	449	**Jean Jeanie** *Fashion FM*
	451	**Laura Ashley** *Fashion F*

Orchard Street | | **North Audley Street**

STORE **MARKS & SPENCER**	458	455	**American Burger** *Restaurant*
National Westminster Bank	466	461	**Mothercare** *Baby store*
Jewellery **H. Samuel**	472	467	**Office** *Shoes FM*
Shoes FM **Peter Lord**	476	469	**Knickerbox** *Underwear*
Fashion F **Etam**	484	471	**Grand Woollen Centre** *Fabrics M & tailor*
Chemist **Boots**	488	473	**Adams** *Children's wear*
Shoes FM **Russell & Bromley**	494	475	**Jacadi** *Children's wear*
Shoes FM **Ravel**	498	479	**Aberdeen Steak House** *Restaurant*
Watches of Switzerland	500	481	**Hennes** *Fashion F*
Shoes FM **Saxone**	502	483	**Oakland** *Fashion M*
		485	**London Jean Company** *Fashion FM*
		487	Alfred Marks *Employment agency*
		487	**Tie Rack** *Fashion M*
		489	**Bay Trading Co** *Fashion M*
		491	**Ryman** *Stationery*
		493	**Dixons** *Cameras & electronics*

Shoes FM **Bally** 468

Portman Street | | **Park Street**

STORE **LITTLEWOODS**	506	499	**Chinacraft** *China & glass*
Fashion FM **Benetton**	522	501	**C&A** *STORE*
Fashion F **Jane Norman**	524	523	**Pizza Hut** *Restaurant*
Fashion F **Next**	526	525	**Stox** *Nick-nacks*
Handbags & luggage **Salisburys**	530	527	**Virgin Records** *Records, CD's & cassettes*
Fashion F **Wallis**	532	537	**Cerex** *Souvenirs*
Fashion F **Evans**	538		

Old Quebec Street

Restaurant **Kentucky Fried Chicken**	542		**Park Lane**
Bureau de change Chequepoint	548		
Marble Arch	●		
Bureau de change Berkeley Credit	550		
Cumberland Hotel	552		
China & glass **Chinacraft**	556		

Great Cumberland Place | | **Marble Arch**

Bond Street – new and old

Oxford Street | | **Oxford Street**

Shoes FM **Dolcis**	87	325	**Next** *Fashion F*
Fashion M **Blazer**	90	81	**Berkertex Brides** *Bridalwear*
Fashion M **Cecil Gee**	92	79	Accountancy Personnel
Restaurant **Old Vienna**	94	77	**Bambino** *Children's wear*
Shoes FM **Grant**	94	76	**Cerruti 1881** *Fashion M*

Blenheim Street

Shoes FM **Kurt Geiger**	95		**Dering Street**
Royal Bank of Scotland	97		
Linens **Frette**	98		
Employment agency Manpower	98	75	**Cerruti 1881** *Fashion M*
Antique restoration **Paul Mitchell**	99	74	**Alexander Juran** *Oriental carpets*
Shoes FM **Alan McAfee**	100	74	**Paul Kaye** *Portrait photographer*
Auctioneers **Phillips**	101	73	**Louis Feraud** *Fashion F*
Jewellers **Nawbar & Co**	102	72	**Timberland** *Fashion M*
Leather goods **Henry's**	103	71	**Etienne Aigner** *Luxury goods, fashion F*
Shoes F **Ivory**	104	70	**Episode** *Fashion F*
Employment agency Reed	104	70	**Kabaret** *Bar*
Fashion F **Laurel**	105	69	**Please Mum** *Childrens' wear*
Fashion F **St John**	106	68	**Carvela** *Shoes F*
Fashion F **Alexon**	107	66	**Escada** *Fashion F*
Fashion F **Lanvin**	108	65	**Bentley & Co** *Jewellers*
Sylvia Lewis Beauty Clinic	108	64	**Dixons** *Cameras & electronics*
Hair salon **Stephen Way Hair**	109		
Shoes FM **Russell & Bromley**	109		

Brook Street

Barclays Bank	111	63	FENWICK *STORE*
Bond Street Silver Galleries	111		
Shoes FM **Bally**	116		
Fashion M **Cecil Gee**	120		
Lane *Fine Art*	123		
Arcade **Bond Street Antiques Centre**	124		
Marriage bureau **Heather Jenner**	124		
Fashion M **Herbie Frogg**	125	53	**Jasons** *Fabrics*
Photography **Wallace Heaton**	126	51	**The White House** *Linen*
Midland Bank	129	50	**Chappell Music Centre**
		49	**Bruno Magli** *Shoes*
		49	**Pinet** *Shoes*

Grosvenor Street

Leather goods **Loewe**	130	46	**Avi Rossini** *Fashion M*
Fashion M **Beale & Inman**	131	46	**Ciao** *Travel*
Fashion F **Beale & Inman**	133	45	**Massada** *Antiques*
Fabrics **Simmonds**	134	43	**Smythson** *Leather goods*
Fashion M **Yves Saint Laurent**	135	42	**Gorgissima** *Fashion F*
Fashion F **Yves Saint Laurent**	137	41	**Mayfair Carpet Galleries**
		38	**Riyahi Gallery** *Fine art*

Bloomfield Place

Fashion F **Marie Claire**	138	37	**Herbie on Bond Street** *Fashion M*
Silver & goldsmiths **S. J. Phillips**	139	36	**Ermenegildo Zegna** *Fashion FM*
Fashion FM **Zilli**	140	36	**Fogal** *Lace*
Antiques **Mallett**	141	34	**Sotheby's** *Auctioneers*
Fashion FM **Polo Ralph Lauren**	143	33	**Richard Green** *Paintings*
Antiques **Frank Partridge**	144	31	**Frank Bolger** *Carpets*
Fine art dealers **Wildenstein**	147	30	**Herbert Johnson** *Milliner FM*
Fine Art Society	148	29	**Gordon Scott** *Shoes FM*
Luggage **Louis Vuitton**	149	28	**Celine** *Accessories F*
Gifts **Isetan**	150	27	**Wana Designs** *Fashion FM*
		26	**Tessiers** *Gold & silversmiths*
		24	**Russell & Bromley** *Shoes FM*

Bruton Street

Conduit Street

Publishers **Time & Life**	155	23a	**Philip Landau** *Fashion M*
Fashion F **Emanuel Ungaro**	153a	23	**Moira** *Antiques*
Luxury goods **Hermes**	155	22	**Moira** *Antiques*
Cashmeres **Ballantyne**	153a	21	**Bruno Piattelli** *Fashion M*
Fashion F **Max Mara**	157	19	**Tecno** *Modern furniture*
Paintings **John Mitchell & Son**	160	18	**Gianni Versace** *Fashion M*
Fashion FM **Valentino**	160	17	**Air India**
Glass **Lalique**	162		
Shoes M **Churches**	163		
Kelly Temporary Services	163		
Fashion FM **Savoy Tailors Guild**	164		

Clifford Street

Grafton Street

		16	**Watches of Switzerland**
Luxury accessories **Asprey**	165	15	**Patek Phillipe** *Watches*
Furriers **Birger Christiansen**	169	15	**George Jensen** *Silversmiths*
Jewellers **Collingwood**	171	14a	**Chopard** *Luxury goods*
Jewellers **Bulgari**	172	14	**Adler of Geneva** *Jewellers*
Fashion F **Karl Lagerfeld**	173	12	**Hennell** *Silversmiths*
Jewellers **Ilias**	174	11	**Philip Antrobus** *Jewellers*
Jewellers **Cartier**	175	10	**Adele Davis** *Fashion F*
Shoes & leatherwear **Rossetti**	177	10a	**Anne Bloom** *Jewellers*
Jewellers **Chaumet**	178	9	**Ciro** *Jewellers*
Jewellers **Ebel**	179	8	**C'est Si Bon** *Fashion F*
Jewellers, gifts **Tiffany & Co**	25	8	**John Mitchell** *Paintings*
Fashion F **Chanel**	26	5	**Rolex** *Watches*
The Royal Arcade	28	4	**Richard Green** *Art gallery*
Silver & jewellery **Holmes**	29	1	National Westminster Bank
Historical Portraits Ltd	30		
Shoes FM **Bally**	30		

Burlington Gardens

Shoes F **Maud Frizon**	31	24	**Ferragamo** *Shoes FM & accessories*
Luxury goods **Gucci**	33	22	**Chatila** *Jewellers*
		20	**Pierre Cardin** *Fashion FM*
		19	**A. Sulka & Co** *Fashion M*
		18	**Alan McAfee** *Shoes M*

Stafford Street

		17	**Rashid** *Carpets*
Fine art **Entwistle**	37	17	**Clough** *Jewellers & pawnbrokers*
Antiques **Deborah Gage**	38	17	**Czechoslovak Travel Bureau**
Marlborough Graphics Gallery	39	16	**Frost & Reed** *Paintings*
Lloyds Bank	39	15	**Rayne House** *Shoes FM*
Employment agency **Success After 60**	40	14	**Colnaghi Galleries** *Paintings*
Fine art **Noortman**	40-41	13	**Leger Galleries** *Paintings*
Fine art **Thos. Agnew & Sons**	43	13	**Benson & Hedges** *Tobacconist*
Fine art **Thomas Gibson**	44	10	**Lufthansa German Airlines**
		10	**Jindo Fur Salon**
		9	**Ginza Yamagataya** *Fashion M*
		7	**Air Nippon Airlines**
		5	**Harvey's** *Antiques*
		4	**Fenzi 19** *Fashion M*
		3	**Belgrave Carpet Gallery**
		2	**ADC Heritage** *Antique silver*
		1a	**F. B. Meyrowitz** *Optician*
		1	**Watches of Switzerland**

Green Park ⊖		**Piccadilly**

South Molton Street

Oxford Street

Left side	No.	No.	Right side
Pub Hog in the Pound Tavern	28	35	Foto Inn Developing & printing
Employment agency Select Appointments	28	36	Bertie Shoes FM
Designer fashion F Browns	23-27	37	Leather Rat Leather fashion FM
Children's wear Benetton 012	22	39	Browns Fashion FM
Bond Street Secretarial Bureau	22	40	Mrs Field's Cookies
Japanese jewellery Electrum	21	41	The Tube Shoes & fashion F
Fashion jewellery Butler & Wilson	20	42	Woodhouse Fashion M
Shoes FM Pied à Terre	19	43	Saga Japanese restaurant
Fashion F Genny	18	43	The Grosvenor Bureau Employment agency
Fashion knitwear FM Joseph Tricot	16	44	French Connection Fashion F
Fashion FM Stefanel	15	45	Browns Fashion FM
Fashion F Joseph	12	45	Optel Employment agency
Designer fashion F Arte	12	46	Widow Applebaum's Jewish restaurant
Adventure Employment	12	47	Hobbs Fashion & shoes FM
Fashion F French for Less	12	48	Grosvenor Gallery
Fashion F Ruby Jones	10	48	Cable & Co Fashion M
Fashion F Pied à Terre	9	49	Skindeep Leather fashions FM
Fashion F Solo	8	50	Pellicano Fashion FM
Fashion FM Benetton	6	52	Trussardi Italian fashion FM
Designer jewellery Andé Bogaert	5	52	The Vestry Fashion FM
Designer jewellery Agatha	4	54	Fabrice Karel Fashion F
Handbags & luggage City Bag Store	3	54	Reed Employment agency
Fashion M Daniel James	2	55	Oliver Fashion M
Shoes FM Podium	1	56	Bang & Olufsen TV & Hi-fi
Restaurant Wheelers	1		

Globe Yard

No.	Right side
57	Adolfo Domínguez Hairdressing salon
57	Molton Brown Hairdressing salon
59	Shane English School
59	Fil à Fil Shirts FM
60	London Business College
60	Vidal Sassoon Hairdressing salon
61	Pineapple Fashion F
63	Pellicano Fashion F
64	South Molton Drug Stores
65	Post Office
66	Ken Lane Jewellers
67	Monsoon Fashion F
68	Crochetta Handknitted fashion F

Regent Street

Left side	No.	No.	Right side
			Great Castle Street
Fashion FM Original Levi's Store	269	214-216	TOP SHOP & TOP MAN STORE
Restaurant Garfunkel's	265		
Underwear Knickerbox	261		
Fashion F Hennes	260		
Oxford Street			Oxford Street
South African Airways	259	266	Waterford/Wedgwood China & glass
Fashion FM Benetton	257	264	Ratners Jewellers
Princes Street		260	Bally Shoes FM
		256	Laura Ashley Fashion F
Chocolates Godiva	247	254	Thorntons Chocolates
Opticians Scrivens Fortifone	245	254	Off the Cuff Shirts FM
Fashion FM House of Scotland	241	246	National Westminster Bank
Posters & cards Cardshops	239		Little Argyll Street
Cameras & film City Photo	239		
Underwear Damart Thermawear	235		
Fashion FM London House	231	244	DICKINS & JONES STORE
Opticians First Sight	229		
Hanover Street			
Building society Woolwich	227		
Irish Airline Aer Lingus	223		
Maddox Street			Great Marlborough Street
Jewellers Pravins	221	214-220	LIBERTY STORE
Telecom Electronics	219	212	Barclays Bank
British salon Tops	217	210	The Gap Fashion FM
Hair salon Alan d	215		
Cyprus Trade & Tourist Centre	213		
Fashion FM Michelle O	207		
Moroccan Tourist Office	205		
China & glass Villeroy & Boch	203		
Conduit Street			Foubert's Place
The Pen Shop	199	204	Jaeger Fashion FM
Fashion FM The Scotch House	191	198	House of Chinacraft China & glass
Jewellery & accessories Carré Blanc	189	188	Hamleys Toys
Jewellers Peter Trevor	189	184	The London House Fabrics & woollens
Israeli airlines El Al	185	178	Just Fax Filofaxes
		176	Kookai Fashion F
New Burlington Place		172	Publishers' Book Clearing Books
		170	Mappin & Webb Jewellers
Noble Furs	183	160	Next Fashion FM, interiors, flowers
Fashion FM R.M.Williams	181	158	Waterford/Wedgwood China & glass
Regent Textiles	181	156	British Airways Travellers Shop
Royal Jordanian Airlines Alia	177		
Cashmeres House of Cashmere	175		
Bureau de change	173		
Saudi Arabia Airlines	171		
Fashion FM Regents	169		

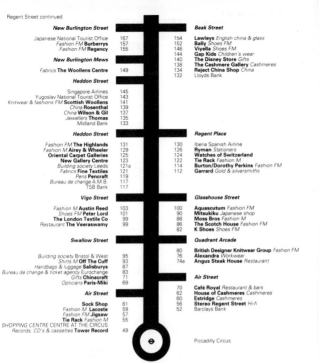

Regent Street continued

Left (West side)	No.	No.	Right (East side)
New Burlington Street			**Beak Street**
Japanese National Tourist Office	167	154	**Lawleys** *English china & glass*
Fashion FM **Burberrys**	157	152	**Bally** *Shoes FM*
Fashion FM **Regency**	155	146	**Viyella** *Shoes FM*
		144	**Gap Kids** *Children's wear*
New Burlington Mews		140	**The Disney Store** *Gifts*
		138	**The Cashmere Gallery** *Cashmeres*
Fabrics **The Woollens Centre**	149	134	**Reject China Shop** *China*
		132	Lloyds Bank
Heddon Street			
Singapore Airlines	145		
Yugoslav National Tourist Office	143		
Knitwear & fashions FM **Scottish Woollens**	141		
China **Rosenthal**	139		
China **Wilson & Gil**	137		
Jewellers **Thomas**	135		
Midland Bank	133		
Heddon Street			**Regent Place**
Fashion FM **The Highlands**	131	130	Iberia Spanish Airline
Fashion M **Airey & Wheeler**	129	126	**Ryman** *Stationers*
Oriental Carpet Galleries	125	124	**Watches of Switzerland**
New Gallery Centre	123	122	**Tie Rack** *Fashion M*
Building society **Leeds**	121a	114	**Burton/Dorothy Perkins** *Fashion FM*
Fabrics **Fine Textiles**	121	112	**Garrard** *Gold & silversmiths*
Pens **Pencraft**	119		
Bureau de change A.M.B.	117		
TSB Bank	117		
Vigo Street			**Glasshouse Street**
Fashion M **Austin Reed**	103	100	**Aquascutum** *Fashion FM*
Shoes FM **Peter Lord**	101	90	**Mitsukiku** *Japanese shop*
The London Textile Co	99	88	**Moss Bros** *Fashion M*
Restaurant **The Veeraswamy**	99	86	**The Scotch House** *Fashion FM*
		82	**K Shoes** *Shoes FM*
Swallow Street			**Quadrant Arcade**
		80	**British Designer Knitwear Group** *Fashion FM*
Building society Bristol & West	95	76	**Alexandra** *Workwear*
Shirts M **Off The Cuff**	93	74a	**Angus Steak House** *Restaurant*
Handbags & luggage **Salisburys**	87		
Bureau de change & ticket agency Eurochange	83		**Air Street**
Gifts **Chinacraft**	71	70	**Café Royal** *Restaurant & bars*
Opticians **Paris-Miki**	69	62	**House of Cashmeres** *Cashmeres*
Air Street		60	**Estridge** *Cashmeres*
		56	**Stereo Regent Street** *Hi-fi*
Sock Shop	61	52	Barclays Bank
Fashion M **Lacoste**	59		
Fashion FM **Jigsaw**	57		
Tie Rack *Fashion M*	55		
SHOPPING CENTRE CENTRE AT THE CIRCUS			
Records, CD's & cassettes **Tower Record**	49		Piccadilly Circus

Kings Road

Left	No.	No.	Right
Sloane Square			**Sloane Square**
STORE **PETER JONES**			⊖ Sloane Square
		7	**Whistles** *Fashion FM*
		7a	**Midas** *Shoes FM*
		9	Post Office
		11	**The Coffee Shop**
		11	**HoHo** *Chinese restaurant*
		13	**Next** *Fashion M*
		15	**Next** *Fashion F*
		17	**Forbuoys** *Newsagents & tobacconists*
		21	Ladbrokes *Turf accountant*
		23	**V. V. Rouleaux** *Ribbons*
		25	Allied-Astors *Employment agency*
Cadogan Gardens		25	Britannia *Employment agency*
		25	**Lazer** *Fashion M*
Children's wear & accessories **Trotters**	34	27	Eurochange *Bureau de change*
Children's playthings **Early Learning Centre**	36	31	**De Ville** *Fashion FM*
Fashion F **Sidney Smith**	36		Duke of York's Headquarters
London School of Bridge	38		
Fashion M **Cecil Gee**	44		
Wine Bar **Blushes**	52		
Natural beauty products **The Body Shop**	54		
Fashion FM **Jeans West**	54		
Restaurant **Pizza Hut**	56		
Chemist **Boots**	58		
Shoes FM **Russell & Bromley**	64		
Sock Shop	68		
Blacklands Terrace			
Fashion FM, home furnishings, **Next**	72		

Lincoln Street

Restaurant **Guys & Dolls**	74
Fashion M **Next**	76
Restaurant **Pizzaland**	80
Fashion M **Simply...**	82
Fashion F **Zoo**	86
Fashion FM **Stefanel**	88
Shoes FM **Cable & Co**	90
Shoes FM **Max Bally**	92
Fashion F **Benetton**	94
Fashion F **Warehouse**	96
Restaurant **The Chelsea Kitchen**	98
Shoes FM **The Tube**	
Fashion FM **Bruce Jeremy**	102

Cheltenham Terrace

33	National Westminster Bank
33a	**Blazer** Fashion M
33c	**Chipie** Fashion M
33d	**Monsoon** Fashion F
33e	**Martins** TV & hi-fi
33f	**Optika** Opticians
33g	**Pied à Terre** Shoes FM
33h	**Our Price** Records

Walpole Street

Anderson Street

Chelsea Building Society	112
Fashion M **Reiss**	114

35	**Safeway** Supermarket

Tryon Street

Fashion FM **The Leather Warehouse**	118
Shoes FM **Bertie**	118
Fashion F **Laura Ashley**	120
SHOPPING MALL KING'S WALK	
Fashion FM **Maglia**	124
Fashion M **Woodhouse**	124a
Shoes FM **Shellys**	124b
Fashion F **Jigsaw**	124c
Fashion FM **Tacchella**	126
Shoes FM **Ravel**	128
Bureau de change **Chequepoint**	130
Children's wear **Benetton 012**	132

Royal Avenue

49	**McDonald's** Restaurant
51	**William Hill** Bookmakers
55	**Pineapple** Fashion F
55	**Arte** Fashion F
59	**Karen Millen** Fashion F

Bywater Street

Beauty products **Crabtree & Evelyn**	134
Fashion FM **Legacy**	136
Building society **Abbey National**	138
Fashion F **Hittite**	138a

Wellington Street

61	Dentics Dentist
63	**Vanilla** Hair & beauty
65	**Sonico Jeans** Fashion FM
67	**Dance** Fashion F
67a	**Strings** Fashion FM
69	**Review** Fashion M

Markham Square

Smith Street

Greetings cards **Post Impressions**	146

69a	**Sissors** Hairdressers
73	**High Five** Fashion M

Fashion FM **XS**	148
Fashion FM **Part Two**	150
Restaurant **The Pheasantry**	150
Restaurant **Mama Bellini's**	150

75	**In Wear** Fashion FM
79	**New Man** Fashion M
81	**Speedway** Fashion FM
83	**A. R. T.** Fashion FM
85	**Marks & Spencer** Foods
87	**Serge** Fashion M
89	**Charcoal** Fashion FM
91	**Good Earth** Chinese restaurant
93	**Office** Shoes FM
95	**Loud** Fashion F
97	**Cotton Club** Fashion F
99	**Woodhouse** Fashion M
105	**Trip** Fashion FM
107	**Stocks** Nightclub
109a	**R. Soles** Leather boots
109	**The Poster Shop**
113	**Rivaaz** Leatherwear FM
115	**Kodo** Fashion F

Markham Street

Stationery **Ryman**	152
Books **Dillons**	152

Jubilee Place

Radnor Walk

Lloyds Bank	164
Fashion FM **Chelsea Leather**	168
Film developers **Snappy Snaps**	170
Chinese restaurant **Choy's**	172
Shoes FM **Blue Velvet**	174
Opticians **Chelsea Eye Centre**	176

119	**Chelsea Potter** Pub & restaurant
121	**The Common Market** Fashion FM
123	**Victoria Wine** Wine Merchants
123a	**Awards** Fashion FM

Burnsall Street

Shawfield Street

Fashion M **Tipo di Moda**	178
Shoes FM **R. Soles**	178a
The Linen Clearance Shop	182
New age gifts **Paradise Farm**	182a
Fashion F **Flying Down To Rio**	184
Fashion FM **Soldier Blue**	184a

127	**Picasso** Restaurant
129	**Slot Machine** Fashion M
135	**Quincy** Fashion M
137	**David Fielden** Fashion F
137	**Antiquarius** Antiques, fashion
139	**Antiquarius** Antiques, fashion
141	**Antiquarius** Antiques, fashion

Flood Street

West side	No.		East side	No.
Dry cleaners **Sketchley**	186		**Jaeger** *Fashion FM*	145
Leather fashion FM **Curio Leather**	186a		**Quarzo** *Fashion FM*	147
Fashion F **Sima**	188a		**Omcar** *Fashion FM*	150
Restaurant **American Burger**	190		**Boy** *Fashion M*	153
Fashion M **GB Classics**	192		**Original Levi's Store** *Fashion FM*	155
Supermarket **Waitrose**	198		Chelsea Methodist Church	155a
Pub **The Trafalgar**	200		**The Penguin Bookshop**	157
Chelsea Cinema	206		**Leather Machine** *Leather fashions FM*	159
Furnishings **Habitat**	206			

Chelsea Manor Street

West side	No.		East side	No.
National Westminster Bank	224		TOWN HALL Citizen's Advice Bureau	179
Post Office	232		**Chenil Galleries**	181
Household goods **Reject Shop**	234		**David Clulow** *Optician*	185
			Photo-Optix *Cameras*	187
			Phlip *Fashion FM*	191
			Henry J Bean's *Bar*	195
			Video Shuttle *Videos*	199
			Amagansett *Fashion M*	201
			Chelsea Audio-Visual Centre	203
			Pucci Pizza *Italian restaurant*	205
			Givans *Linen*	207

Sydney Street

COUNCIL OFFICES 250

Dovehouse Street

CHELSEA FIRE STATION

Oakley Street

Manresa Road

Glebe Place

KING'S COLLEGE LONDON

East side	No.
Tiger Tiger *Toys*	219
My Old Dutch *Restaurant*	221
Naf-Naf *Fashion FM, children's wear*	229
Café Tempo *Restaurant*	235
Chelsea Food Fayre	237

Bramerton Street

Carlyle Square

East side	No.
Designers Sale Studio *Fashion F*	241
Encore! *Dress agency FM*	245
Antique Market	245
Joanna Booth *Antiques*	247
S. Borris *Delicatessen*	251
Chelsea Antique Market	253
Green & Stone *Artists' materials*	259
Soho Interior Design	263
Isaac T. Lloyd *Chemist*	267
David Pettifer *Antiques*	269
Designers Guild *Furnishings*	271
The Stockpot *Restaurant*	271b
David Tron *Antiques*	275
Designers Guild *Fabric & wallpapers*	277

West side	No.
Estate agents De Groot Collis	296
Pub **Cadogan Arms**	298

Church Street / **Old Church Street**

West side	No.		East side	No.
National Westminster Bank	300		Cannon Cinema	279
Interior designers **Osborne & Little**	304		Mr Light *Lighting*	279
Antiques **Godson & Coles**	310		Europa Foods *Supermarket*	279
Restaurant **Le Gourmet**	312		Delcor *Interiors*	279c
Artists' materials **Chelsea Art Stores**	314		Brats *Gifts & cards*	281
Restaurant **Mario & Franco**	316		Gianni Barbato *Shoes FM*	285
Maps & prints **Old Church Galleries**	320		Raffles *Club*	287
Picture framing **Alfred Hecht**	324		Sasha Hetherington *Evening wear F*	289
Carpets **Bernadout**	328		The Jam *Restaurant*	289a
Restaurant **Lo Spuntino**	330		Joanna's Tent *Fashion FM & children's wear*	289
Restaurant **Big Easy**	334			
Antiques **Monro Heywood**	336			
Furniture **William Yeoward**	336			
Chinese restaurant **Ming**	338			
Fabrics **Liberty Prints**	340a			
Restaurant **Thierry's**	342			
Antiques **Tony Buzzi**	344			
Barclays Bank	348			

Paultons Square

The Vale

East side	No.
Hooper & Purchase *Antique furniture*	303
Bamboo Kitchen *Chinese take-away food*	305
Ciancimino International *Furniture*	307
Kriston *Hand-finished launderers*	309
Chelsea Rare Books	313
Stephen King *Fashion M*	315
Gregor Schumi *Hairdressers*	317
J. & F. E. Simpson *Jewellers*	319
Rococo *Chocolates*	321
Robot *Shoes & fashion M*	323

West side	No.
Sportswear **Million Dollar Sports**	350
Fashion M **Nigel Hall**	350
Designer fashion FM, hairdresser, bar **The Garage**	350
Wellworth Food & Wines	350
Fashion M **Daniel James**	352
National Westminster Bank	352a

Beaufort Street

EATING & DRINKING

Restaurants

These have been chosen for authentic food and good cooking. For more detailed information on where and what to eat see Nicholson's London Restaurant Guide.
The Restaurant Switchboard – 081-888 8080 – offers free up-to-the-minute information and advice on London's restaurants – 09.00-20.00 Mon-Sat.

The following price guide refers to a three-course meal for one including VAT but without wine:

£ - £10.00 and under
££ - £10.00-£20.00
£££ - £20.00-£30.00
£££+ - £30.00 and over

(Reserve) - advisable to reserve
Open to . . . - last orders

A - Access/Mastercard/Eurocard
Ax - American Express
Dc - Diners Club
V - Visa/Barclaycard

B - Breakfast
L - Lunch
D - Dinner

Service charge*: many restaurants add service on to the bill, usually at 12½%, but do not always say so – if in doubt ask. However, they do usually say if service is not included.*

AFRICAN & CARIBBEAN
Afric-Carib
1 Stroud Green Rd N4. 071-263 7440. Restaurant and take-away specialising in spicy Nigerian dishes. Chicken, beef or fish with plantains and yams. Relaxed, informal atmosphere. *LD open to 23.00.* A.V. **£**

The Calabash   4 F3
38 King St WC2. 071-836 1976. In the basement of the Africa Centre. Masks and African textiles adorn the walls. Regional dishes include beef with green bananas and coconut cream, chicken and groundnut stew. *LD open to 22.30. Closed Sun & L Sat.* A.Ax.Dc.V. **££**

AMERICAN
Chicago Pizza Pie Factory   4 C2
17 Hanover Sq W1. 071-629 2669. American deep-pan pizzas surrounded by Chicago paraphernalia including tapes of the local radio station and US football videos flown in weekly. *LD open to 23.30, to 22.30 Sun.* No credit cards. **£**

Hard Rock Café   4 C5
150 Old Park Lane W1. 071-629 0382. Ever popular hamburger joint, just off Hyde Park Corner. Vast room on two levels with good quality food and non-stop rock. Occasional queues outside. *LD open to 24.15, to 24.45 Fri & Sat.* No credit cards. **££**

Joe Allen   4 F3
13 Exeter St WC2. 071-836 0651. In a converted Covent Garden warehouse, this London branch follows the pattern of its New York and Paris counterparts. Cocktail bar and blackboard menu of steaks, hamburgers, ribs and chilli followed by cheesecake or brownies. Fashionably crowded, especially after the theatre. *LD (Reserve) open to 24.45, to 24.00 Sun.* No credit cards. **££**

Smollensky's Balloon   4 D4
1 Dover St W1. 071-491 1199. Big, light and bustling restaurant and bar on two floors. Generous portions – speciality is steaks, with a choice of seven sauces. Rich desserts – chocolate mousse, peanut butter cheesecake. *LD open to 24.00, to 22.30 Sun.* A.Ax.Dc.V. **££**

CENTRAL EUROPEAN
Kerzenstüberl   4 B2
9 St Christopher's Place W1. 071-486 3196. Authentically Austrian with dishes such as leberknoedel soup, Viennese goulash accompanied by accordion music, dancing and singing. *LD (Reserve) open to 23.00. Licensed to 01.00. Closed Sun & L Sat.* A.Ax.Dc.V. **££**

Old Vienna Budapest   4 C3
94 New Bond St W1. 071-629 8716. Lavishly decorated, traditional Austrian restaurant. Menu covers specialities from Austria and Hungary – expect to be serenaded at your table by the resident singer! *LD open to 01.00, to 22.30 Sun.* A.Ax.Dc.V. **££**

St Moritz   4 E3
161 Wardour St W1. 071-734 3324. Two floors rigged out like a ski hut in the famous Swiss resort. Cheese and beef fondues are the house speciality. *LD (Reserve) open to 23.30. Closed Sun & L Sat.* A.Ax.Dc.V. **££**

CHINESE
Dragon Gate   4 E3
7 Gerrard St W1. 071-734 5154. The first and probably best

Szechuan restaurant in London. Sliced pork with garlic and chilli, tea-smoked duck. Pancakes or almond curd to follow. *LD open to 23.15.* A.Ax.Dc.V. **££**

Ken Lo's Memories of China   **7 A2**
67-69 Ebury St SW1. 071-730 7734. The windows are etched with Tang dynasty horses and the menu features regional specialities: Shanghai sea bass, Szechuan crispy beef, Cantonese seafood with black bean sauce. *LD open to 23.00. Closed Sun.* A.Ax.Dc.V. **£££+**

Lee Ho Fook   **4 E3**
15-16 Gerrard St W1. 071-734 9578. Renowned Cantonese cooking, very popular with the local Chinese. Huge portions at reasonable prices. Dim sum at *lunchtime. LD open to 23.30, to 22.30 Sun.* A.Ax.Dc.V. **££**

Poons   **4 E3**
4 Leicester Sq WC2. 071-437 1528. Wind-dried meats are a speciality at this unpretentious, family-run Cantonese restaurant. Also unlicensed branch at 27 Lisle St WC2 (**4 E3**) 071-437 4549. *LD (Reserve) open to 23.30. Closed Sun.* No credit cards. **££**

EAST EUROPEAN
Borshtch N'Tears   **3 G6**
46 Beauchamp Place SW3. 071-589 5003. Crowded, informal and lively Russian restaurant. Borshtch, beef Stroganoff, chicken Dragomiroff and blinis served to the accompaniment of Russian music. *D open to 01.00.* Ax. **££**

Daquise   **6 D2**
20 Thurloe St SW7. 071-589 6117. Polish restaurant popular with Polish émigrés. Serves traditional, simple and inexpensive dishes: borshtch, bigor and sausages. Also afternoon tea with excellent pastries. *LD open to 23.30.* No credit cards. **£**

Gay Hussar   **4 E2**
2 Greek St W1. 071-437 0973. Intimate, cosy, much-loved Hungarian restaurant. Try the stuffed cabbage, chilled wild cherry soup, pike with beetroot sauce. *LD (Reserve) open to 22.45. Closed Sun.* Ax. **££**

Luba's Bistro   **3 F6**
6 Yeoman's Row SW3. 071-589 2950. Authentic Russian cooking in down-to-earth, spartan surroundings. Sit at long tables and bring your own wine. Beef Stroganoff, kooliebaiaka (salmon pie), zrazra (chicken with vegetables), golubtsy, pojarsky. *D open to 23.00. Closed Sun.* A.Ax.V. **££**

ENGLISH
Baker & Oven   **1 C6**
10 Paddington St W1. 071-935 5072. In a converted Victorian

bakery, with the original bakers' ovens still used to cook good, simple food in generous quantities. Soups, pies, roasts and pheasant in season. *LD (Reserve) open to 22.30. Closed Sun & L Sat.* A.Ax.Dc.V. **££**

Baron of Beef   **5 D2**
Gutter Lane EC2. 071-606 6961. First-class food served in great comfort. Roast Scotch beef, braised oxtail, steak and oyster pie. Fine wine list and notable clarets. *LD (Reserve) open to 20.00. Closed Sat & Sun.* A.Ax.Dc.V. **£££+**

English House   **6 F2**
3 Milner St SW3. 071-584 3002. Intimate restaurant in the style of an English country house. Classic English cooking. *LD (Reserve) open to 23.30, to 22.00 Sun.* A.Ax.Dc.V. **£££+**

Porters   **4 F3**
17 Henrietta St WC2. 071-836 6466. Large, pillared dining room lined with old carvings and mirrors. Imaginative, good value English fare in the form of pies – Billingsgate, lamb and apricot, turkey and chestnut. Bread and butter pudding, rhubarb crumble or Stilton to follow. Also traditional Sunday lunch. *LD open to 22.30.* A.V. **££**

Rules   **4 F3**
35 Maiden Lane WC2. 071-836 5314. Something of a landmark, rich in associations – Dickens, Thackeray, Edward VII and Lillie Langtry all dined here. Jugged hare, steak and kidney pie, grouse and venison. On the tourist circuit so booking essential. *LD (Reserve) open to 24.00. Closed Sun.* A.Ax.Dc.V. **£££**

Simpson's-in-the-Strand   **4 F3**
100 Strand WC2. 071-836 9112. An English institution with an Edwardian club atmosphere. Excellent fish and meat dishes – smoked salmon, Dover sole, duck or saddle of mutton. Fine wines and vintage port. Booking and correct dress essential. *LD (Reserve) open to 23.00. Closed Sun.* A.Ax.Dc.V. **£££**

Tiddy Dols   **4 C4**
55 Shepherd Market W1. 071-499 2357. Unique, comfortable restaurant spreading over several houses dating from 1741. Low ceilings and winding staircases abound. Fillet of venison, beef Wellington, cock-a-leekie and the original gingerbread Tiddy Dol on the menu. Live entertainment. *D (Reserve) open to 23.30.* A.Ax.V. **£££**

FISH
Bentley's   **4 D3**
11-15 Swallow St W1. 071-734 4756. Famous seafood restaurant and oyster bar. Wide variety of fish, plus excellent oysters, prawns and crab. *LD (Reserve) open to 23.00. Closed Sun.* A.Ax.Dc.V. **£££**

Overton's   **7 B1**
4-6 Victoria Bldgs, Terminus Place SW1. 071-834 3774. Also at 5 St James's St SW1 (**4 D4**) 071-839 3744. Long-established fish restaurant with an olde-world atmosphere. Oysters, lobster, Dover sole. *LD (Reserve) open to 22.30. Closed Sun.* A.Ax.Dc.V. **£££**

Sweetings   **5 D3**
39 Queen Victoria St EC4. 071-248 3062. Tiny 150-year-old City eatery. Excellent service and very popular so queueing often necessary. *L open to 15.00. Closed Sat & Sun.* No credit cards. **££**

Wheeler's Old Compton Street   **4 E2**
19 Old Compton St W1. 071-437 2706. Old-established and popular chain of restaurants specialising in expertly cooked fish dishes. Welcoming yet sophisticated atmosphere. Scallops, lobster Normande, sole Egyptian and shellfish. Several other branches. *LD (Reserve) open to 23.00.* A.Ax.Dc.V. **£££**

FRENCH
Ark   **3 C4**
122 Palace Gdns Terrace W8. 071-229 4024. Also at 35 Kensington High St W8 (**3 B6**) 071-937 4294. Cosy and friendly atmosphere with good French provincial food. Onion soup, noisette d'agneau, foie de veau. *LD (Reserve) open to 23.15. Closed L Sun.* A.V. **££**

Boulestin   **4 F3**
1a Henrietta St WC2. 071-836 7061. Famous old restaurant opened in the 1920s. Club-like atmosphere with a menu offering sumptuous dishes such as crabe à l'artichaut, balottine de turbot farcie au homard, tulipe de sorbets. Fine wines, dignified service. *LD open to 23.15. Closed Sun & L Sat.* A.Ax.Dc.V. **£££+**

Claridges Restaurant   **4 C3**
Brook St W1. 071-629 8860. Distinguished French cooking in luxurious surroundings. The atmosphere is typical of the sedate thirties. Polished service and a notable wine list. *LD (Reserve) open to 24.00.* A.Ax.Dc.V. **£££+**

L'Epicure   **4 E2**
28 Frith St W1. 071-437 2829. Confident, flamboyant establishment with excellent French cuisine. Speciality is flambés, also steak maison, crêpes suzette and kidneys in marsala. *LD (Reserve) open to 23.15. Closed Sun & L Sat.* A.Ax.Dc.V. **£££**

L'Escargot   **4 E2**
48 Greek St W1. 071-437 6828. A Soho institution. Brasserie on the ground floor offers reasonably priced and varied dishes, upstairs the French restaurant is more formal. Menu changes

every two months. Excellent wine list. *LD (Reserve) open to 23.15. Closed Sun & L Sat.* A.Ax.Dc.V. **£££**

Le Gavroche 4 B3
43 Upper Brook St W1. 071-408 0881. One of the best restaurants in London, renowned for its luxurious atmosphere and imaginative *haute cuisine*. Cooking and service faultless. *LD (Reserve) open to 23.00. Closed Sat & Sun.* A.Ax.Dc.V. **£££+**

Langan's Brasserie 4 C4
Stratton St W1. 071-493 6437. Vast room with a carefully contrived atmosphere of decaying splendour. One of London's most fashionable eating places (co-owned by Michael Caine). Excellent classic French cuisine from a small menu. *LD (Reserve) open to 23.30. Closed Sun & L Sat.* A.Ax.Dc.V. **£££**

Mon Plaisir 4 F2
21 Monmouth St WC2. 071-836 7243. Small, typically French restaurant. Short, unpretentious menu; escalope à la crème, coq au vin. Friendly atmosphere and helpful service. *LD (Reserve) open to 23.15. Closed Sun & L Sat.* A.Ax.Dc.V. **££**

GREEK, TURKISH & CYPRIOT

Beotys 4 F3
79 St Martin's Lane WC2. 071-836 8768. Comfortable establishment with authentic Greek cooking. Stuffed vine leaves, kalamarakia (squid cooked in its own ink), moussaka, baklava and kadeifi. Perfect for an after-theatre dinner. *LD open to 23.30. Closed Sun.* A.Ax.Dc.V. **£££**

Mega Kalamaras 3 C3
76 Inverness Mews W2. 071-727 9122. Also smaller and less expensive **Mikro Kalamaras** 66 Inverness Mews W2. 071-727 9122. True taverna atmosphere. Superb national dishes ranging from dolmades to baklava. Bouzouki players on some evenings and dancing. *D (Reserve) open to 24.00 (Mikro to 23.30). Closed Sun.* A.Ax.Dc.V. **££**

White Tower 4 E1
1 Percy St W1. 071-636 8141. Elegant, first class cuisine in London's first Greek restaurant. Lengthy menu and refined atmosphere; moussaka, shashlik and duck with bulghur. *LD (Reserve) open to 22.30. Closed Sat & Sun.* A.Ax.Dc.V. **£££**

INDIAN

Bombay Brasserie 6 C2
Bailey's Hotel, 140 Gloucester Rd SW7. 071-370 4040. Large, fashionable restaurant decorated in colonial style. Representative dishes from several regions including Bombay thali, Goan fish curry. *LD (Reserve D) open to 24.00.* A.Ax. L **££** D **£££**

Khan's 3 C2
13-15 Westbourne Grove W1. 071-727 5420. Vast room with

oriental arches and palm tree pillars. Cheap, cheerful and noisy with excellent north Indian cuisine. *LD (Reserve D) open to 24.00.* A.Ax.Dc.V. **£**

Last Days of the Raj   **4 F2**
22 Drury Lane WC2. 071-836 1628. Bengali specialities in crowded theatreland restaurant. Meat thali, lamb tandoori, hot and sour chicken. *LD (Reserve) open to 23.30. Closed L Sun.* A.Ax.Dc.V. **££**

Red Fort   **4 E2**
77 Dean St W1. 071-437 2115. Widely regarded as one of the best Indian restaurants in London. Warm pink decor, tropical greenery and soft lighting create a palatial atmosphere in which to try Moghul Indian dishes. Quails in mild spice, chicken korahi, tandooris and nan breads. Cocktail bar. *LD (Reserve) open to 23.15.* A.Ax.Dc.V. **££**

Veeraswamy's   **4 D3**
99-101 Regent St (entrance in Swallow St) W1. 071-734 1401. Excellent, authentic food in atmosphere of a pre-war Indian club. Traditionally dressed waiters, and a large choice of curries – Moglai, Delhi, Madras, Ceylon and Vindaloo. *LD (Reserve) open to 23.15, to 22.00 Sun.* A.Ax.Dc.V. **££**

INEXPENSIVE EATING
The following are places where you can eat a good meal for **£10.00 or under**. The café serving 'sausage, egg and chips' is not included here, neither are the international fast food chains which can be found on nearly every High Street. This list prizes distinctive or unusual cooking and atmosphere – but particularly good value for money.

Bistro Vino   **6 D2**
1 Old Brompton Rd SW7. 071-589 3888. Also at 5 Clareville St SW7 (**6 C2**) 071-373 3903. Separately managed but similar style informal restaurants. Good simple bistro food at very reasonable prices in cheerful, lively surroundings. *LD open to 23.45.* (Clareville St *D only*). A.V. **£**

Chelsea Kitchen   **6 E3**
98 King's Rd SW3. 071-589 1330. Part of the Stockpot group. The daily menu offers a good choice of hot, cheap dishes. Soup, moussaka, spaghetti. Licensed. *LD open to 23.45.* No credit cards. **£**

Ed's Easy Diner   **4 E2**
12 Moor St (off Old Compton St) W1. 071-439 1955. Also at 362 King's Rd SW3 (**6 B6**) 071-352 1956. American-style diner with counter-top jukeboxes and bar seating. Hamburgers and fries dominate, but also club sandwiches and salads. US imported beers, thick milkshakes and malts. *LD open to 24.00, to 01.00 Fri & Sat.* No credit cards. **£**

Geales   **3 B4**

2-4 Farmer St W8. 071-727 7969. Large selection of excellent fish and chips. Cod's roe, clams, sole. Licensed. *LD open to 23.00. Closed Sun & Mon.* A.V. **£**

The Lantern

23a Malvern Rd NW6. 071-624 1796. Amazing variety and quality at low prices. French bistro with simple, candlelit ambience, soft music, blackboard menu and wine list. Predictably busy. *LD (Reserve Fri & Sat) open to 24.00, to 23.00 Sun.* A.V. **£**

My Old Dutch   **4 G1**

131 High Holborn WC1. 071-242 5200. Traditional Dutch farm-house decor, pine tables and chairs. Over 100 generous sized pancakes, some savoury, some sweet. *LD open to 23.30, to 24.30 Fri & Sat.* A.Ax.Dc.V. **£**

Pizza Express   **1 G6**

30 Coptic St WC1. 071-636 2244. Modern pizza parlour with a large oven in the middle, so you can see you pizza being cooked. Many varieties. Numerous branches. Live jazz at 10 Dean St W1 (**4 E2**) 071-437 9595. *LD open to 24.00.* A.Ax.V. **£**

Spaghetti House   **4 E3**

24 Cranbourn St WC2. 071-836 8168. Genuine Italian spaghetti house, friendly and busy. Soups, pasta dishes, pastries and ice-cream. Several branches. Disco at Vecchia Milano, 74-77 Welbeck St W1 (**4 C2**) 071-935 2371. *LD open to 23.00. Closed Sun.* A.Ax.Dc.V. **£**

Standard   **3 C2**

23 Westbourne Grove W2. 071-727 4818. Large, popular Indian restaurant serving over 80 specialities including tandoori and vegetarian dishes. *LD (Reserve) open to 24.00.* A.Ax.Dc.V. **£**

Stockpot   **4 E3**

40 Panton St SW1. 071-839 5142. Also at 6 Basil St SW3 (**3 G5**) 071-589 8627. Crowded, noisy and excellent value. Home-made soups, casseroles and puddings. *LD open to 23.00, to 22.00 Sun* (Basil St *closed Sun*). No credit cards. **£**

Wong Kei   **4 E3**

41-43 Wardour St W1. 071-437 8408. Large, cheap and cheer-ful Cantonese restaurant on four floors. Always busy and bustling, don't expect courteous service but do expect to have to share a table! *LD open to 23.15.* No credit cards or cheques. **£**

INTERNATIONAL

Ménage à Trois   **3 F6**

14-15 Beauchamp Place SW3. 071-584 9350. Starters (some very elaborate) and desserts only in this smart establishment. Scotch lobster, crudités, caviar, ménage à trois – pastry parcels of cheese or seafood. Summer pudding, ice-cream daquiris, terrine of chocolate. *LD (Reserve) open to 23.30. Closed Sun & L Sat.* A.Ax.Dc.V. **£££**

Neal Street Restaurant   **4 F2**
26 Neal St WC2. 071-836 8368. Chic and modern with elegantly prepared dishes culled from international recipes. Prawns wrapped in bacon, scrambled egg with smoked eel, roast duck with apple sauce. *LD (Reserve) open to 23.00. Closed Sat & Sun.* A.Ax.Dc.V. **£££**

Pomegranates   **7 C4**
94 Grosvenor Rd SW1. 071-828 6560. Highly original and adventurous restaurant. Good value, set price menu is an amalgam of international dishes including Creole, West Indian, Chinese, French and Italian influences. Multi-national wine list. *LD (Reserve D) open to 23.15. Closed Sun & L Sat.* A.Ax.Dc.V. L **££** D **£££**

ITALIAN
Biagi's   **3 G2**
39 Upper Berkeley St W1. 071-723 0394. Well-run, intimate trattoria decorated with fishing nets. Good varied Italian dishes. Scallopine alla crema, entrecôte alla pizzaiola, saltimbocca. *LD (Reserve) open to 23.00.* A.Ax.Dc.V. **££**

Kettners   **4 E3**
29 Romilly St W1. 071-437 6437. There has been a restaurant here since the mid-19thC. Sumptuous interior, probably the most pleasant setting for pizzas and hamburgers (now owned by the Pizza Express chain). Champagne bar. Pianist *every evening. LD (no reservations) open to 24.00.* A.Ax.Dc.V. **££**

Leoni's Quo Vadis   **4 E2**
26-29 Dean St W1. 071-437 4809. One of Soho's oldest and most famous restaurants, in the same building where Karl Marx once lived. Excellent traditional cuisine; fettucine Quo Vadis, with cream, tomato and fresh basil, is one of the favourites. *LD (Reserve) open to 23.15, to 22.30 Sun.* A.Ax.Dc.V. **£££**

Luigi's   **4 F3**
15 Tavistock St WC2. 071-240 1795. Something of an institution, often crowded and popular with after-theatre diners. Photographs of entertainment personalities decorate the walls. Good, authentic food: cannelloni, grilled mussels, veal and chicken dishes. *LD (Reserve) open to 23.30. Closed Sun.* A.Dc.V. **£££**

San Lorenzo   **3 G6**
22 Beauchamp Place SW3. 071-584 1074. One of London's best known Italian restaurants offering excellent traditional cuisine. Fashionable clientele enjoy the unusual veal and chicken dishes. Extensive wine list. Outdoor seating in summer. *LD (Reserve) open to 23.30. Closed Sun.* No credit cards. **£££**

JAPANESE
Hiroko 3 A4
Hilton International Hotel Kensington, 179 Holland Park Ave W11. 071-603 5003. Courteous staff, traditional cuisine. Sashimi (raw fish), sankaiyaki (thin slices of beef and chicken with prawns and oysters) cooked at the table. A la carte or set menus. *LD (Reserve) open to 22.00. Closed L Mon.* A.Ax.Dc.V. **£££+**

Masako 4 B2
6-8 St Christopher's Place W1. 071-935 1579. Authentic Japanese restaurant with private dining rooms attended by charming waitresses in kimonos. Wide-ranging menu including set sukiyaki and tempura meals. *LD open to 22.00. Closed Sun.* A.Ax.Dc.V. **£££+**

JEWISH
Bloom's 5 G2
90 Whitechapel High St E1. 071-247 6001. Also at 130 Golders Green Rd NW11. 081-455 1338. Bustling kosher restaurants, offering large helpings of gefilte fisch, lockshen pudding, meatballs, salt beef, stuffed kishka. *LD open to 21.30. Closed Sat, Jewish hols & D Fri.* A.Ax.V. **££**

Widow Applebaum's 4 C3
46 South Molton St W1. 071-629 4649. American-Jewish deli offering 101 dishes. Mirrors and photos of New York in the jazz age and wooden benches outside for *summer* eating. Matzo balls, hot salt beef and pastrami, apfelstrüdel and ice-cream sodas. *LD open to 19.30. Closed Sun & D Sat.* No credit cards. **£**

KOREAN
Arirang 4 D2
31-32 Poland St W1. 071-437 9662. Green and white decor, lacquered vases and a bamboo ceiling. Waitresses in Korean dress steer you through the large menu which may include kim chee (hot pickled cabbage), yuk kwe (beef strips with pear). Sake and ginseng to drink. *LD (Reserve) open to 23.00. Closed Sun.* A.Ax.Dc.V. **££**

Shilla 4 D2
58-69 Great Marlborough St W1. 071-434 1650. Charming service to help you with the speciality here – barbecue dishes. Delicious sauces accompany beef, chicken or seafood. Set menus available. *LD open to 23.00.* A.Ax.Dc.V. **££**

MEXICAN
La Cucaracha 4 E2
12-13 Greek St W1. 071-734 2253. London's first Mexican restaurant, in the cellars of a converted monastery. Hacienda-

style decor with a sunny covered terrace at the back. Ceviche, tacos, burritos, enchiladas. *LD open to 23.30.* A.Ax.Dc.V. **££**

Los Locos   **4 F3**
24 Russell St WC2. 071-379 0220. Also at 14 Soho St W1 (**4 E2**) 071-287 0005. Mexican bar and restaurant with lots of Tex-Mex specials. Nachos, tacos, carnitas, steaks, enchiladas, fajitas cooked over mesquite wood. Mexican beers and cocktails. Disco from *23.30 every night. D open to 03.00.* A.Ax.Dc.V. **££**

MODERN EUROPEAN
Alistair Little   4 E2
49 Frith St W1. 071-734 5183. Fashionable restaurant with an imaginative, frequently changing menu. Tempting, delicious results such as tomato and basil soup, noisettes of lamb with exotic fungi. *LD (Reserve) open to 23.00. Closed Sun & L Sat.* A.V. **£££**

Bibendum   6 E2
81 Fulham Rd SW3. 071-581 5817. Delightful restaurant within the unusual 1910 Michelin building. Long menu of simple, elegant and inventive French and English dishes. Carefully chosen wine list. *LD (Reserve) open to 23.30, to 22.30 Sun.* A.V. **£££+**

Chanterelle   6 C3
119 Old Brompton Rd SW3. 071-373 5522. Attractive, atmospheric decor in this popular, busy restaurant. Good value set menus may include mousse of Stilton and Armagnac, trout marinated in white wine. *LD (Reserve) open to 23.30.* A.Ax.Dc.V. L **£** D **££**

Odin's   1 D6
27 Devonshire St W1. 071-935 7296. Stylish, luxurious and decorated with interesting photographs, prints and paintings. Frequently changing à la carte menu may include red mullet pâté, stuffed roast duck, rack of lamb. *LD (Reserve) open to 23.15. Closed Sun & L Sat.* Ax.V. **£££**

OPEN-AIR EATING
Barbican, Waterside Café   2 E6
Level 5, Barbican Centre EC2. 071-638 4141. Modern self-service café by the man-made lake of the arts centre. Snacks or full meals. *LD open to 20.00.* No credit cards. **£-££**

Dan's   6 E3
119 Sydney St SW3. 071-352 2718. Bright, airy room with hanging plants and seating in a rear garden. English and French cuisine. Try the warm spinach mousse with basil coulis, rack of lamb with honey and mustard. *LD open to 22.30. Closed L Sat.* A.Ax.Dc.V. L **££** D **£££**

La Famiglia   **6 C4**
7 Langton St SW10. 071-351 0761. Attractive, with pretty rear garden and southern Italian cooking. Fourteen types of pasta available. Italian wines. *LD open to 23.30.* A.Ax.Dc.V. **£££+**

New Serpentine Restaurant   **3 G4**
Hyde Park W2. 071-402 1142. A charming waterside restaurant/café in Hyde Park, run by Prue Leith and serving a tempting menu of Modern European dishes plus teas and snacks. Tables on the terrace in *summer. LD open to 22.30.* A.V. **£-£££**

SCANDINAVIAN
Anna's Place
90 Mildmay Park N1. 071-249 9379. Small, intimate restaurant in Anna's home serving excellent Scandinavian and French food. Camembert with parsley, gravadlax, beef or herring, duck breast with Swedish cabbage. *LD (Reserve) open to 22.45. Closed Sun & Mon.* No credit cards. **££**

Garbo's   **1 B6**
42 Crawford St W1. 071-262 6582. Pleasant pink restaurant serving Scandinavian home cooking. Herring salad Baltic, cabbage stuffed with minced pork, beef and rice or smoked eel. Imported Swedish beers and Schnapps. *LD (Reserve) open to 23.30. Closed Sun & L Sat.* A.Ax.Dc.V. **££**

SOUTH EAST ASIAN
Desaru   **4 E3**
60-62 Old Compton St W1. 071-734 4379. A very busy Indonesian/Malaysian restaurant, convenient for the theatre. Choice of set menus to help those in a hurry. Good noodle dishes and specialities. *LD open to 23.45, to 22.00 Sun.* A.Ax.Dc.V. **££**

Melati   **4 E3**
1 Great Windmill St W1. 071-437 2754. Very popular Indonesian restaurant serving rice and noodle dishes, meat and seafood specialities. Fried rice with shredded chicken and shrimps, fish cutlets in coconut sauce. *LD (Reserve) open to 23.30. Closed Sun.* A.Ax.Dc.V. **££**

Rasa Sayang   **4 E2**
10 Frith St W1. 071-734 8720. Unpretentious restaurant offering authentic Singaporean, Indonesian and Malaysian food. Try the beef satay, prawns, gado gado. *LD (Reserve D) open to 23.30. Closed L Sat.* A.Ax.Dc.V. **£££**

SPANISH & PORTUGUESE
Caravela   **3 F6**
39 Beauchamp Place SW3. 071-581 2366. Small, intimate

basement Portuguese restaurant. The menu is largely seafood, with fresh grilled sardines, prawns piri piri and regional specialities. Wine list exclusively Portuguese. Live music in the *evening. LD (Reserve) open to 01.00, to 24.00 Sun. Closed L Sun.* A.Ax.Dc.V. **£££**

Valencia   **6 A4**
1 Empress Approach, Lillie Rd SW6. 071-385 0039. London's oldest Spanish restaurant. Large menu of regional dishes and wine list strong on Rioja and Catalan wines. Guitarist *every night. D open to 24.15.* A.V. **££**

THAI
Bahn Thai   **4 E2**
21a Frith St W1. 071-437 8504. Stylish decor and high-quality authentic Thai food including unusual dishes such as silver pomfret in chilli. Vegetarians well catered for. Fiery Thai whisky to drink. *LD (Reserve) open to 23.15.* A.Ax.V. **££**

Blue Elephant   **6 A5**
4-5 Fulham Broadway SW6. 071-385 6595. One of London's best Thai restaurants. The surroundings resemble a tropical jungle, the perfect backdrop for excellent, beautifully prepared dishes presented by waiters in Thai costume. *LD (Reserve) open to 24.30, to 22.30 Sun.* A.Ax.Dc.V. **£££+**

Busabong Too   **6 C4**
1a Langton St SW10. 071-352 7414. Low tables and cushions to sit on. Very pleasant, attentive service. Fisherman's soup, beef satay, mint pork with water chestnuts. *LD (Reserve) open to 24.00. Closed L Sat & Sun.* A.Ax.Dc.V. **££**

VEGETARIAN & WHOLEFOOD
Many restaurants now cater for vegetarian tastes, with a variety of dishes on their menus. Below are two specialist establishments:

Cranks   **4 D2**
8 Marshall St W1. 071-437 9431. The original London health-food restaurant. Hot and cold vegetable dishes, soups, pies, salads, cakes, bread, and vegetable juices. Licensed. Other branches. *LD (Reserve D) open to 23.00. Closed Sun.* A.Ax.Dc.V. **££**

Diwana Bhel-Poori House   **1 E5**
121 Drummond St NW1. 071-387 5556. Also at 50 Westbourne Grove W2 (**3 C2**) 071-221 0721. Indian vegetarian food at very reasonable prices. Samosas, thalis, bhajis. *LD open to 23.45. Closed Mon.* A.Dc.V. **£**

VIETNAMESE
Mekong   **7 C2**
46 Churton St SW1. 071-630 9568. Sample a blend of

Vietnamese and Chinese cuisine in this simple bistro-like restaurant. Spring rolls, beef with lemon grass and a variety of vegetarian dishes. Set menus. *LD (Reserve) open to 23.00.* A.V. **££**

Van Long   **4 E2**
40 Frith St W1. 071-434 3772. Attractive, modern Vietnamese restaurant with pretty, pastel decor. Excellent soups and seafood dishes. Long menu but set meals help the uninitiated. *LD open to 23.15.* A.Ax.Dc.V. **££**

Breakfast and brunch

Price symbols for this section only are: **£** *under £5.00;* **££** *£5.00-£8.00;* **£££** *over £8.00.*

CAFÉS
Bar Italia   **4 E2**
22 Frith St W1. 071-437 4520. Authentic Italian café, serving breakfast all day. *Open 07.00-very late (at least 04.00).* No credit cards. **£**

Bartholomew's   **5 C1**
57a West Smithfield EC1. 071-606 3903. Traditional English breakfast. *Open 07.00-11.00. Closed Sat & Sun.* A.Ax. Dc.V. **££**

The Hermitage   **1 G4**
19 Leigh St WC1. 071-387 8034. Friendly, stylish café. Baguettes, croissants, pain au chocolat. Newspapers provided. *Open 10.00-23.00.* V. **£**

Le Tire Bouchon   **4 D3**
6 Upper James St W1. 071-437 5348. Continental breakfast. *Open 08.00 (breakfast until 11.00)-21.30. Closed Sat & Sun.* A.Ax.Dc.V. **££**

HOTELS
Claridge's   **4 C3**
Brook St W1. 071-629 8860. English, à la carte or Continental. *Served 07.30-10.00.* A.Ax.Dc.V. **££-£££**

Hyde Park, Park Room   **4 A5**
66 Knightsbridge SW7. 071-235 2000. English, à la carte or Continental. *Served 07.00-10.00 (08.00-11.00 Sun & Bank hols).* A.Ax.Dc.V. **£££**

Ritz   **4 D4**
Piccadilly W1. 071-493 8181. English, à la carte or Continental. *Served 07.30-10.30.* A.Ax.Dc.V. **£££**

Savoy   **4 G3**
Strand WC2. 071-836 4343. English or Continental. *Served 07.30 (08.00 Sun)-10.30.* A.Ax.Dc.V. **£££**

Afternoon tea

Afternoon tea is a British institution; at one time very fashionable, sociable, leisurely and gossipy. This list gives some of the remaining strongholds. Prices can vary but you should not normally expect to pay more than £12.00 for a full tea. Most will cost between £5.00-£10.00.

HOTELS
Brown's   **4 D3**
Albemarle St W1. 071-493 6020. Very English, country house setting. Sandwiches, cakes, muffins. *Served 15.00-18.00.*

Claridge's   **4 C3**
Brook St W1. 071-629 8860. A touch of class in the comfortable reading room. Sandwiches, assorted pastries, cakes. *(Reserve) Served 15.00-17.15.*

Dorchester   **4 B4**
Park Lane W1. 071-629 8888. Dainty sandwiches, cakes and pastries in opulent surroundings. *Served 15.00-17.45.*

Ritz   **4 D4**
Piccadilly W1. 071-493 8181. Tea in the Palm Court, with dainty sandwiches, pastries and cream cakes. *Served 15.15 & 16.30.*

DEPARTMENT STORES
Most large department stores provide afternoon tea but the following are among the best:

Fortnum & Mason   **4 D4**
181 Piccadilly W1. 071-734 8040. Afternoon tea is available at three locations in the store *Mon-Sat*. St James's Restaurant serves a set tea of sandwiches, scones, cake, tea or coffee to a piano accompaniment *15.00-17.20*. The Patio Bar and Soda Fountain offer an à la carte tea menu *14.30-17.00*.

Harrods Georgian Restaurant   **3 G6**
Knightsbridge SW1. 071-730 1234. Enjoy a buffet of tea, coffee or fruit juice with bread and butter, scones, cakes and pastries while listening to the pianist. *From 15.45.* Alternatively have tea served on the Terrace *from 15.30.*

CAFÉS
Maison Bouquillon   **3 C3**
45 Moscow Rd W2. 071-727 0373. Over 50 varieties of cream cakes and pastries. Also hot savoury dishes, croissants. *Open 08.30-21.00 Mon-Fri, to 20.00 Sat & Sun.* No credit cards.

Maison Sagne   **1 C6**
105 Marylebone High St W1. 071-935 6240. Traditional tea

shop with its own bakery and delicious pâtisserie. Coffee and croissants, lunches and tea. *Open 09.00-17.00, to 12.30 Sat. Closed Sun.* No credit cards.

Pâtisserie Valerie   **4 E3**
44 Old Compton St W1. 071-437 3466. Soho pâtisserie with excellent cakes and sandwiches. *Open 08.00-21.30. Closed Sun.* No credit cards.

THÉ DANSANT

Waldorf Hotel   **4 G3**
Aldwych WC2. 071-836 2400. Opulent Pancock tea lounge with comfort and good service. Edwardian elegance. Dancing to the band and full set tea *Fri-Sun 15.30-18.30.*

Brasseries

Here is a selection of establishments serving food all day *(from breakfast to full meals):*

La Brasserie   **3 F6**
272 Old Brompton Rd SW3. 071-584 1688. Very like a true French brasserie. Conventional menu with omelettes, croque monsieur, also breakfast and pâtisseries. *Open 08.00-24.00 Mon-Sat, 10.00-24.00 Sun.* A.Ax.Dc.V. **££**

Covent Garden Brasserie   **4 F3**
1 Covent Garden Piazza WC2. 071-240 6654. Relaxed atmosphere at this Parisian style brasserie. Breakfast and afternoon tea as well as light meals and more substantial dishes. *Open 11.00-23.00.* A.Ax.Dc.V. **££**

The Dôme   **6 D4**
354 King's Rd SW3. 071-352 7611. One of a chain of French-style brasseries based on the Paris Dôme. Coffee, wine, spirits, beer and good food from breakfast and pâtisseries to steak sandwiches. *Open 08.00-23.00.* A.Ax.Dc.V. **££**

Soho Soho   **4 E2**
11-13 Frith St W1. 071-494 3491. A brasserie/wine bar with a selection of good value wines. Brasserie offers typical French menu with croque monsieur etc; Rôtisserie downstairs offers grills and snacks all day. *Open 12.00-23.00. Closed Sun.* A.Ax.Dc.V. **££**

Wine bars

Most wine bars are open pub hours: 11.00/11.30-15.00 & 17.30-23.00 Mon-Sat; 12.00-14.00 & 19.00-22.30 Sun. *Some are open all day:* 11.00-23.00 Mon-Sat; 12.00-14.00 & 19.00-22.30 Sun. *These are denoted by* 🍷.
Most offer cold food (such as sandwiches) all day, and bar

food (anything from pâté to steak) at designated times at lunchtime and in the evening.
L = 12.00/12.30-14.30/15.00.
D = 18.00-22.30/23.00.
all day = throughout the day from lunchtime to last orders in the evening.
Nicholson's London Restaurant Guide *gives more detailed information on brasseries and wine bars in the capital.*

Andrew Edmunds　　　　　　　　　　　　　**4 D3**
46 Lexington St W1. 071-437 5708. Small, charming wine bar/restaurant serving excellent wines and imaginative food. *L D.*

🍷 **Archduke**　　　　　　　　　　　　　　　**5 B4**
Concert Hall Approach, South Bank SE1. 071-928 9370. Nestling underneath the arches near Waterloo Station, with pleasant green decor, live jazz and good food. The restaurant specialises in sausages from around the world. *L D.*

🍷 **L'Artiste Musclé**　　　　　　　　　　　　**4 C4**
1 Shepherd Market W1. 071-493 6150. Informal, French wine bar. Good food with daily specials chalked up on the blackboard. Reasonably priced, mainly French, wines. Tables outside in *summer. L D.*

Balls Bros
One of the oldest wine bar chains in London. Very popular, with most of its branches in the City. Over 60 wines on their list, plus wines by the glass. All the following serve food *lunchtime* and *evening.* NB: All branches *close early at 20.30/21.00 and are closed Sat & Sun.* The following is only a selection:

🍷 Hay's Galleria, Tooley St SE1. 071-407 4301.　　**5 F4**
3 Budge Row, Cannon St EC4. 071-248 7557. *L only.*　**5 D2**
2 Old Change Court, St Paul's Churchyard EC4.　　**5 D2**
071-248 8697.
St Mary-at-Hill EC3. 071-626 0321.　　　　　　**5 F3**
6 Cheapside EC2. 071-248 2708.　　　　　　　**5 D2**

🍷 **Bill Bentley's Wine Bar**　　　　　　　　　**3 G6**
31 Beauchamp Place SW3. 071-589 5080. Dark, cosy bar with an old-fashioned interior and an excellent fish restaurant upstairs. Snacks from the oyster bar and a reasonably priced wine list. *L D. Closed Sun.*

🍷 **Bow Wine Vaults**　　　　　　　　　　　　**5 D2**
10 Bow Churchyard EC4. 071-248 1121. Victorian bar within the sound of Bow Bells. Popular with City gents, with a good selection of over 100 French, Californian, Spanish and German wines. Imaginative food. *L only. Open to 20.30. Closed Sat & Sun.*

🍷 **Brahms & Liszt**　　　　　　　　　　　　　**4 F3**
19 Russell St WC2. 071-240 3661. Lively, crowded wine bar

with loud music and a friendly atmosphere. Good food and a reasonable selection of wines. Food *all day. Closed D Sun.*

Café des Amis du Vin   **4 F3**
11-14 Hanover Place WC2. 071-379 3444. Close to the Royal Opera House and always busy. Good range of French, German and Spanish wines accompanied by an inventive menu. *L D. Closed Sun.*

Cork & Bottle   **4 E3**
44-46 Cranbourn St WC2. 071-734 7807. Spacious basement wine bar with an unusual variety of quality wines. *L D.*

🍷 **Crusting Pipe**   **4 F3**
27 Covent Garden Piazza WC2. 071-836 1415. Part of the Davy's chain. Very popular with seating outside under the piazza canopy. Grills and daily specials in the restaurant and very friendly, helpful service. Food *all day. Closed Sun.*

Davy's Wine Bars
Old prints and sawdust-covered floors create a bygone Victorian image in these wine bars, the names of which date back to the wine trade of 100 years ago. All branches offer a good selection of wines and a range of food (see individual entries). NB: Most branches *close early at around 20.30 and are closed Sat & Sun.* The following is only a selection:

Boot & Flogger   **5 D5**
10-20 Redcross Way SE1. 071-407 1184. Food *all day.*

Bung Hole   **4 G1**
57 High Holborn WC1. 071-242 4318. *L.*

City Boot   **5 E1**
7 Moorfields High Walk EC2. 071-628 2360. *L.*

Dover Street Wine Bar   **4 C3**
8-9 Dover St W1. 071-629 9813. A basement wine bar with a friendly atmosphere and a very good selection of wines. Live music. Open late for real night owls! *L D. Open to 03.00. Closed Sun & L Sat.*

🍷 **Ebury Wine Bar**   **7 A2**
139 Ebury St SW1. 071-730 5447. Crowded and cramped, but with a pleasant atmosphere. Comprehensive wine list. *L D.*

🍷 **Gordon's**   **4 F4**
47 Villiers St WC1. 071-930 1408. 200-year-old wine bar in curved, cavernous undervaults. Excellent selection of wines and sherries. Good food. *L D.*

🍷 **Shampers**   **4 D3**
4 Kingly St W1. 071-437 1692. A brasserie and wine bar with a congenial atmosphere and fine selection of wines. Good, imaginative menu. *L D.*

El Vino   **5 B2**
47 Fleet St EC4. 071-353 6786. Something of an institution. Thoroughly masculine atmosphere popular with local lawyers

and still adhering to a dress code – men in jacket and tie and women in dresses/skirts. Long and famous wine list. *L D. Open to 20.00. Closed Sat & Sun.*

Pubs

Some pubs still operate under the following opening hours: 11.00/11.30-15.00 & 17.30-23.00 Mon-Sat; 12.00-14.00 & 19.00-22.30 Sun. Others are open all day 11.00-23.00 Mon-Sat; 12.00-14.00 & 19.00-22.30 Sun. These are denoted by 🍺 *Most pubs serve sandwiches and cold snacks all day, but hot food at designated times at lunchtime and in the evening.*
In the following section:
Bar food = ploughmans, salads, sandwiches, pies, lasagne.
Restaurant = three-course menu and more substantial dishes.
L = 12.30-14.30.
D = 17.30-21.00/22.00:
Nicholson's London Pub Guide *gives more detailed information on where to drink in the capital.*

🍺 Admiral Codrington   6 E2
17 Mossop St SW3. 071-589 4603. Wood-panelled, gaslit house with a good range of malt whiskies. Big garden with overhanging grape vine. Bar food *L* Restaurant *L.*

The Cartoonist   5 B2
76 Shoe Lane EC4. 071-353 2828. In the heart of the .old newspaper world, this Victorian pub is the headquarters of the International Cartoonist Club and wallpapered with cartoons! Bar food *L D. Closed Sat & Sun.*

🍺 Cheshire Cheese   5 B3
5 Little Essex St WC2. 071-836 2347. Intimate Jacobean pub with original beams and three bars. Regulars come from the nearby Law Courts and it is reputedly haunted by an unfriendly ghost! Bar food *L. Closed Sat & Sun.*

🍺 Dirty Dick's   5 F2
202 Bishopsgate EC2. 071-283 5888. The original pub named after Nat Bentley, well-known 18thC miser of the ballad. The cobwebs, stuffed cats and other detritus have since been removed with the remnants preserved behind glass. Bar food *L* Restaurant *L.*

The Flask
77 Highgate West Hill N6. 081-340 3969. Famous 17thC tavern named after the flasks bought here and filled at the Hampstead wells. Dick Turpin once hid in the cellars. Former patrons include Hogarth. and Karl Marx. Bar food *L D* Restaurant *L.*

🍺 French House   4 E2
49 Dean St W1. 071-437 2799. Refuge for the Free French during World War II. De Gaulle drank here, as have Maurice

Chevalier, Brendan Behan and Dylan Thomas. Excellent choice of wines and champagnes. Bar food *L D*.

🍺 George Inn   5 D5
77 Borough High St SE1. 071-407 2056. Unique galleried coaching inn rebuilt 1676 and featured in Dickens' *Little Dorrit*. Courtyard entertainment (usually Shakespeare) in *summer*. Wine bar. Restaurant. Bar food *L D* Restaurant *L D*.

Holly Bush
22 Holly Mount, off Heath St NW3. 071-435 2892. Picturesque and rambling pub dating to 1796. Unchanged atmosphere prevails with gas lamps and a dark, sagging ceiling. Bar food *L D*.

Island Queen   2 D3
87 Noel Rd N1. 071-226 5507. Looming papier mâché figures dominate the bar in this popular local. Pool room and restaurant. Bar food *L* Restaurant *Fri, Sat & Sun only D*.

The Lamb   2 B5
94 Lamb's Conduit St WC1. 071-405 0713. A busy Bloomsbury local with some intriguing music-hall photographs and Hogarth prints. Original snob-screens. Bar food *L D* Restaurant *Sun only L D*.

🍺 Lamb & Flag   4 F3
33 Rose St WC2. 071-497 9504. 300-year-old pub originally called the 'Bucket of Blood' because of the occurrence of bare fist fights (Dryden apparently got the 'once over' here). Now a popular, mellow bar. Fine range of cheeses. Bar food *L*.

Old Bull & Bush
North End Way NW3. 081-455 3685. The famous pub of the Florrie Forde song. Drink on the forecourt and gaze at Hampstead Heath opposite. Bar food *L* Restaurant *L*.

Running Footman   4 C4
5 Charles St W1. 071-499 2988. Once had the longest name in London, 'I am the only Running Footman' (after the men who used to run before carriages, clearing the way and paying the tolls). Popular with nearby workers. Bar food *L D* Restaurant *D*.

🍺 The Salisbury   4 F3
90 St Martin's Lane WC2. 071-836 5863. Glittering Edwardian pub in the heart of theatreland. Cut-glass mirrors and first-class hot and cold buffet. Famous meeting place for theatre people. Bar food *L D*.

Seven Stars   5 B2
53 Carey St WC2. 071-242 8521. Behind the Law Courts stands this early 17thC pub, one of the smallest in London. Bar food *L*.

🍺 Sherlock Holmes   4 F4
10 Northumberland St WC2. 071-930 2644. Upstairs is a perfect replica of Holmes' study at 221b Baker St. Bar food *L D*.

🍺 Spaniard's Inn
Spaniard's Rd NW3. 071-455 3276. Famous 16thC inn with literary and Dick Turpin associations. Pretty garden. Bar food *L D*.

Still & Star   **5 G2**
1 Little Somerset St (off Mansell St) E1. 071-488 3761. The only one of its name in England, and set in 'blood alley' where Jack the Ripper struck. Bar food *L* Restaurant *L D*.

RIVERSIDE PUBS
🍺 The Anchor   **5 C3**
Bankside SE1. 071-407 1577. 18thC replacement of original destroyed by Great Fire of 1666. Exposed beams, large open fireplace. Bar food *L D* Restaurant *L D (Reserve)*.
The Angel
101 Bermondsey Wall East SE16. 071-237 3608. 15thC Thames side pub on piles, with extensive views of Tower Bridge, the City and the Pool of London. Famous former imbibers include Samuel Pepys, Captain Cook and Laurel and Hardy. Bar food *L D* Restaurant *L D*.
Bull's Head
Strand-on-the-Green W4. 081-994 0647. 350-year-old Chiswick waterfront tavern. Cromwell was nearly caught here by the Royalists. Sheltered beer garden and terrace. Bar food *L D*.
🍺 Cutty Sark
Ballast Quay, Lassell St SE10. 081-858 3146. Quiet Georgian pub with wooden interior. Overlooks the river and wharves near *Cutty Sark* in dry dock. Bar food *L D* Restaurant *D*.
🍺 Dickens Inn   **5 G4**
St Katharine's Way E1. 071-488 2208. Converted historic warehouse with fine views of the diverse craft in St Katharine's Dock marina. Outside eating in *summer*. Two restaurants. Bar food *L D* Restaurant *L D*.
🍺 The Dove
19 Upper Mall W6. 081-748 5405. Mellow 18thC pub with terrace overlooking the river. Graham Greene and Ernest Hemingway drank here. Has the smallest bar room, which has earned it an entry in the *Guinness Book of Records*. Bar food *L D* Restaurant *L D*.
London Apprentice
62 Church St, Old Isleworth, Middx. 081-560 1915. Famous 16thC pub with fine Elizabethan and Georgian interiors. Prints of Hogarth's *Apprentices*. Bar food *L D* Restaurant *L D*.
🍺 The Mayflower
117 Rotherhithe St SE16. 071-237 4088. Partially rebuilt Tudor inn named after the ship in which the Pilgrim Fathers reached America. The only pub in England licensed to sell British and American stamps. Drink on the jetty in good weather. Bar food *L* Restaurant *L D*.
Prospect of Whitby
57 Wapping Wall E1. 071-481 1095. Historic dockland tavern

with many famous and infamous associations. Decorated with nautical souvenirs and fine pewter. Restaurant overlooking the river. Bar food *L D* Restaurant *L D.*

MUSIC PUBS
These vary enormously from pubs with a pianist playing old favourites to those with large audience space for live bands. The pubs listed below are all established live music venues. It's always advisable to check listings in advance to find out what is on. Most pubs with a separate music room charge an entry fee, though it is rarely more than £5.00 and often less.

Bull & Gate
389 Kentish Town Rd NW5. 071-485 5358. Jazz, R & B or blues. *Evenings Mon-Sun.* Bar food *D.*

● Bull's Head
373 Lonsdale Rd SW13. 081-876 5241. Modern jazz by top English and international musicians. *Evenings Mon-Sun & Sun lunchtime.* Bar food *D* Restaurant *L D.*

Half Moon
93 Lower Richmond Rd SW15. 081-788 2387. Jazz, R & B, rock, folk and soul in separate back room. Occasional top names. Bar food *D.*

Swan Tavern   6 A5
1 Fulham Broadway SW6. 071-385 1840. Mixed bands and R & B *evenings Mon-Sat & Sun lunchtime.* Bar food *D.*

White Lion   3 E4
37 Central St EC1. 071-253 4975. Traditional East End pub where you can sing along to the piano played *evenings Fri-Mon & Sun lunchtime.* Bar food *L D.*

THEATRE PUBS
Gate at the Prince Albert   3 B3
11 Pembridge Rd W11. 071-229 0706. New works, adaptations of novels and revivals of lesser known plays by important writers. Performances *Mon-Sat.*

King's Head   2 D3
115 Upper St N1. 071-226 1916. Probably the best known and most widely reviewed of the theatre pubs. Decorated with theatre bills. You can have a meal before the show and stay at your table for the performance. Live music also. Performances *Mon-Sat.* Restaurant *L D.*

Latchmere Theatre   6 F6
503 Battersea Park Rd SW11. 071-223 3549. Good reputation for plays, cabaret and reviews. Check listings in *Time Out* or *What's On* for late-night shows and Sunday performances. Performances *Mon-Sat.*

ENTERTAINMENT

For more detailed information see Nicholson's London Nightlife Guide.
Artsline: *071-388 2227 offers free advice and information on access to arts and entertainment for disabled people.*

Theatre ticket agencies

Fenchurch Booking Agency   5 D4
94 Southwark St SE1. 071-928 8585.
Keith Prowse
071-581 6600. Tickets for most major concerts and shows.
Society of West End Theatre Half-Price   4 E3
Ticket Booth (SWET)
Leicester Sq WC2. Unsold tickets are sold at half price on the day of the performance from this red, white and blue pavilion. *Open 11.00-12.00* (matinées only) *& 14.00-18.00.*
Ticketmaster UK Ltd   4 F3
78 St Martin's Lane WC2. 071-379 4444.

Theatres

Adelphi   4 F3
Strand WC2. 071-836 7611. Musicals including the long-running *Me and My Girl.*
Albery   4 F3
St Martin's Lane WC2. 071-867 1115. Originally the New Theatre. Renamed in 1973. Musicals, comedy and drama.
Aldwych   4 G3
Aldwych WC2. 071-836 6404. Former London home of the Royal Shakespeare Company. Offers a wide programme of plays, comedies and musicals.
Ambassadors   4 E3
West St WC2. 071-836 6111. Small theatre, the original home of *The Mousetrap.*
Apollo   4 E3
Shaftesbury Ave W1. 071-437 2663. Old tradition of musical comedy. Now presents varied productions, including musicals, comedy and drama.
Apollo Victoria   4 C6
17 Wilton Rd SW1. 071-828 8665. This auditorium was completely transformed to accommodate the hit rollerskating railway musical *Starlight Express.*

Barbican 2 E6

Barbican Centre, Barbican EC2. 071-638 8891. Purpose-built for the Royal Shakespeare Company; the main auditorium is for large-scale productions in repertory and the Pit, a smaller studio theatre, is for new works.

Comedy 4 E3

Panton St SW1. 071-930 2578. Good intimate theatre showing unusual comedy and small-cast plays.

Drury Lane (Theatre Royal) 4 G3

Catherine St WC2. 071-836 8108. Operated under Royal Charter by Thomas Kiligrew in 1663, it has been burnt or pulled down and rebuilt four times. Nell Gwynne performed here and Orange Moll sold her oranges. Garrick, Mrs Siddons, Kean and others played here. General policy now is vast productions of musical plays.

Duchess 4 G3

Catherine St WC2. 071-836 8243. Opened 1929. Plays, serious drama, light comedy and musicals.

Duke of York's 4 F3

St Martin's Lane WC2. 071-836 5122. Built by 'Mad (Violet) Melnotte' in 1892. Associated with names like Frohman, George Bernard Shaw, Granville Barker, Chaplin and the Ballet Rambert. Refurbished by the present owners, Capital Radio, for major productions.

Fortune 4 F3

Russell St WC2. 071-836 2238. Small compared with its neighbour, Drury Lane. Intimate revues (Peter Cook and Dudley Moore shot to fame here in *Beyond the Fringe*), musicals and modern drama.

Garrick 4 E2

Charing Cross Rd WC2. 071-379 6107. Built 1897. Notable managers included Bouchier and Jack Buchanan.

Globe 4 E3

Shaftesbury Ave W1. 071-437 3667. A wide variety of successful plays and comedies. The third theatre of this name in London.

Greenwich

Crooms Hill SE10. 081-858 7755. Stages a season of eight plays annually including new works, revivals and classics, often with famous names in the cast. Bar and restaurant.

Haymarket (Theatre Royal) 4 E3

Haymarket SW1. 071-930 9832. Originally built in 1721 as the Little Theatre in the Hay, it became Royal 50 years later. The present theatre was built by Nash in 1821 and is sometimes enlivened by the ghost of Mr Buckstone, Queen Victoria's favourite actor-manager. He no doubt approves of the policy to present plays of quality.

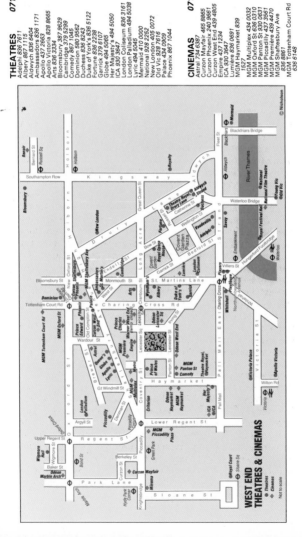

THEATRES 071-

Adelphi 836 7611
Albery 867 1115
Aldwych 836 6404
Ambassadors 836 1171
Apollo 437 2663
Apollo Victoria 828 8665
Arts 836 3334
Bloomsbury 387 9629
Cambridge 379 5299
Comedy 867 1045
Duchess 836 8243
Duke of York's 836 5122
Fortune 836 2238
Garrick 379 6107
Globe 494 5065
Her Majesty's 494 5050
ICA 930 3647
London Coliseum 836 3161
London Palladium 494 5038
Lyric 494 5045
Mermaid 410 0000
National 928 2252
New London 405 0072
Old Vic 928 7616
Palace 434 0909
Phoenix 867 1044

Piccadilly 867 1118
Players 839 1134
Playhouse 839 4401
Prince Edward 734 8951
Prince of Wales 839 5972
Queen's 494 5040
Royal Court 730 1745
Royal Festival Hall 928 8800
Royal Opera House 240 1066
Royalty 242 9136
St. Martin's 836 1443
Savoy (temp. closed) 836 8888
Shaftesbury 379 5399
Strand 240 0300
Theatre Royal, Drury Lane 836 8108
Theatre Royal, Haymarket 930 8800
Vaudeville 836 9987
Victoria Palace 834 1317
Whitehall 867 1119
Wigmore Hall 935 2141
Wyndham's 867 1116
Young Vic 928 6363

CINEMAS 071-

Astral 734 6387
Curzon Mayfair 465 8865
Curzon Phoenix 240 9661
Curzon West End 439 4805
Empire 437 1234
ICA 930 3647
Lumiere 836 0691
MGM Haymarket 839 1527
MGM Multiplex 434 0032
MGM Oxford St 636 0310
MGM Panton St 930 0631
MGM Piccadilly 437 3561
MGM Premiere 439 4470
MGM Shaftesbury Ave 836 8861
MGM Tottenham Court Rd 636 6148

Metro 437 0757
Minema 235 4225
National Film Theatre 928 3232
Odeon Haymarket 839 7697
Odeon Leicester Sq 930 6111
Odeon Mezzanine (Odeon Leicester Sq) 930 6111
Odeon Marble Arch 723 2011
Odeon West End 930 5252
Plaza 437 1234
Prince Charles 437 8181
Renoir 837 8402
Warner West End (temp. closed)

WEST END
THEATRES & CINEMAS

© Nicholson

Her Majesty's   4 E3
Haymarket SW1. 071-839 2244. A fine Victorian baroque
theatre founded by Beerbohm Tree. Successes include *West
Side Story, Fiddler on the Roof, Amadeus* and *Phantom of the
Opera.*

London Palladium   4 D2
8 Argyll St W1. 071-437 7373. Second in size to the Coliseum,
it houses top variety shows and the annual Royal Command
Performance.

Lyric   4 E3
Shaftesbury Ave W1. 071-437 3686. Oldest theatre in
Shaftesbury Avenue (built 1888). Eleonora Duse, Sarah
Bernhardt, Owen Nares and Tallulah Bankhead all had long
runs here.

Lyric Hammersmith
King St W6. 081-741 2311. Rebuilt and restored to original
Victorian splendour inside a modern shell. Spacious foyers,
bar, restaurant and terrace. Wide-ranging productions.

Mermaid   5 C3
Puddle Dock, Blackfriars EC4. 071-236 5568. Plays and
musicals. Restaurant and two bars overlooking the Thames.

National   5 A4
South Bank SE1. 071-928 2252. Complex of three theatres,
the Olivier, Lyttelton and Cottesloe. Home of the National
Theatre Company. Stages a wide mixture of plays in repertory,
including new works, revivals, Shakespeare and musicals.
Also free foyer entertainment. Restaurants, bars, exhibitions.

New London   4 F2
Drury Lane WC2. 071-405 0072. Can convert from a 900-seat
conventional theatre to an intimate, theatre-in-the-round within
minutes. Built on the site of the old Winter Gardens. The hit
musical *Cats* is well-established here.

Old Vic   5 B5
Waterloo Rd SE1. 071-928 7616. Built 1818. For a long time
the home of the National Theatre Company, then housed the
Prospect Theatre Company. It now shows plays and musicals
amid recreated Victorian decor.

Palace   4 E3
Shaftesbury Ave W1. 071-434 0909. Listed building. Originally
intended by Richard D'Oyly Carte to be the Royal English
Opera House, but eventually became the Palace Theatre of
Varieties. Staged performances by Pavlova and Nijinski and
became a musical comedy house in the 1920s. *Jesus Christ
Superstar* and *Les Miserables* both had record runs here.

Phoenix   4 E2
Charing Cross Rd WC2. 071-867 1044. A large theatre showing comedies, plays and musicals.

Piccadilly   **4 D3**
Denman St W1. 071-867 1118. A pre-war theatre which
showed the first season of 'Talkies' in Britain. Varied post-war
history of light comedy, plays and musicals.

Playhouse   **4 F4**
Northumberland Ave WC2. 071-839 4401. Edwardian theatre
used as a BBC studio and then closed in 1975. Restored to
former glory and re-opened in 1987. Stages musicals, serious
drama and comedies.

Prince Edward   **4 E3**
Old Compton St W1. 071-734 8951. Started life as the
'London Casino' in 1936 and has also been a cinema. Now a
large theatre staging musicals. The hit show *Evita* ran for 2900
performances.

Prince of Wales   **4 E3**
Coventry St W1. 071-839 5989. Rebuilt 1937, this large,
modern theatre has housed many musicals.

Queen's   **4 E3**
Shaftesbury Ave W1. 071-734 1166. Very successful between
the wars. Still presents good drama and varied productions.

Royal Court   **6 F2**
Sloane Sq SW1. 071-730 1745. Home of the English Stage
Company, which produces many major experimental plays.

St Martin's   **4 E3**
West St WC2. 071-836 1443. Intimate playhouse with unusual
polished teak doors. *The Mousetrap* continues its record run
here having transferred from the Ambassadors.

Savoy   **4 G3**
Strand WC2. 071-836 8888. Entrance is in the forecourt of
the Savoy Hotel. Produces a variety of plays, comedies and
musicals. *Temporarily closed due to fire damage.*

Shaftesbury   **4 E3**
Shaftesbury Ave WC2. 071-379 5399. Permanent base of the
Theatre of Comedy Company.

Strand   **4 G3**
Aldwych WC2. 071-240 0300. Large theatre presenting a
mixture of straight plays, comedies and musicals.

Vaudeville   **4 F3**
Strand WC2. 071-836 9987. Listed building which originally ran
farce and burlesque (hence the name), then became straight,
which for the most part it remains.

Victoria Palace   **4 D6**
Victoria St SW1. 071-834 1317. Musicals, variety shows and
plays. Once home of the Crazy Gang and the 'Black and White
Minstrel Show'.

Westminster   **4 D6**
Palace St SW1. 071-834 0283. Arts centre opened in 1931,
but now a general theatre. Plays and musicals.

Whitehall   **4 F4**
14 Whitehall SW1. 071-867 1119. Closed down in 1983, reopened in 1986 with the interior restored to its full art deco splendour. Now one of the Wyndham Theatres group staging varied productions.

Wyndham's   **4 E2**
Charing Cross Rd WC2. 071-867 1116. Small, pretty and successful theatre founded by Sir Charles Wyndham, the famous actor-manager. Plays, comedy and musicals.

Young Vic   **5 B5**
66 The Cut SE1. 071-938 6363. Young people's repertoire theatre mainly showing the classics and established modern plays, but also some new plays and musicals.

Open-air theatre

Various parks in London stage one-off theatrical events in summer. To find out more about these, check Time Out *and* What's On *or phone the individual park (see* Out and About *on p61). The two below have permanent open-air theatres:*

Court Theatre   **3 A5**
Holland Park W8. 071-602 7856. 600-seat theatre staging dance, opera and theatre productions *Jun-Aug.* Canopy covering is a definite attraction given the fickleness of the English summer! *Phone for times and days.*

Regent's Park Open-Air Theatre   **1 C4**
Inner Circle, Regent's Park NW1. 071-486 2431. Enclosed within the park, in a magical setting. Plays by Shakespeare (*A Midsummer Night's Dream* is a perennial favourite) and others alternate from *May-Sep.* Book in advance. *Performances 20.00 Mon-Sat & 14.30 Wed, Thur, Sat.*

Opera, ballet and dance

London Coliseum   **4 F3**
St Martin's Lane WC2. 071-836 3161. London's biggest theatre – 2356 seats. A leading national music venue, home of the English National Opera and a favourite with visiting foreign companies. Dance and ballet productions are staged in *summer*, opera at other times. Box office *open 10.00-20.00. Closed Sun.* A.Ax.Dc.V.

The Place   **1 F4**
17 Duke's Rd WC1. 071-387 0031. One of the most innovative and modern dance venues. It is home to the London Contemporary Dance School and London Contemporary Dance Theatre, which stages interestingly choreographed productions. Box office *open 12.00-18.00, or up until time of performance.* A.V.

Royal Opera House   4 F3
Covent Garden WC2. 071-240 1066. Recorded information:
071-836 6903. Credit card booking: (0898) 600001. The home
of the Royal Ballet and the Royal Opera Company is the most
lavish theatre in London and the greatest stage for British
opera and ballet. Sixty-five tickets are reserved for sale at the
box office in Floral St from *10.00* on the day of the performance only (except for gala performances). If the performance
is a sell-out, 50 standing-room tickets are made available in the
foyer at *19.00*. Be warned – queues have been known to start
at dawn! Box office *open 10.00-20.00. Closed Sun.* A.Ax.Dc.V.

Sadler's Wells   2 C4
Rosebery Ave EC1. 071-278 8916. The first theatre here was
a 'musick' house built in 1683 by Thomas Sadler as a side
attraction to his medicinal well. Birthplace of the English
National Opera, it now stages productions by leading British and
international ballet, dance and opera companies. Box office
open 10.30-19.30, or 18.30 if no performance. A.Ax.Dc.V.

Concert halls

Barbican Hall   2 E6
Barbican Centre EC1. 071-628 8795. Base of the London
Symphony Orchestra. Three one-month seasons per year.
Also used as a venue for opera, jazz, and light classical music.
Box office *open 09.00-20.00 Mon-Sun.* A.Ax.V.

Central Hall   4 E5
Storey's Gate SW1. 071-222 8010. This ornate building is the
Chief Methodist Church, built 1905-11. Its large hall – seating
2640 – is used for organ recitals and orchestral concerts. Box
office *open 09.00-17.00 Mon-Sun.* No credit cards.

Conway Hall   2 B6
Red Lion Sq WC1. 071-242 8032. Two halls, one of which is
famous for hosting celebrated *Sun eve* chamber music concerts from *Oct-Apr*. No box office. No credit cards.

Purcell Room   5 A4
South Bank SE1. 071-928 8800. Smallest of the three South
Bank concert halls. Popular and ideal for chamber music and solo
concerts. Box office *open 10.00-20.00 Mon-Sun.* A.Ax.Dc.V.

Queen Elizabeth Hall   5 A4
South Bank SE1. 071-928 8800. Shares a foyer with the
Purcell Room. Seats 1100, and usually stages chamber music,
small orchestral concerts or solo recitals. Box office *open
10.00-20.00 Mon-Sun.* A.Ax.Dc.V.

Royal Albert Hall   3 E5
Kensington Gore SW7. 071-589 8212. Victorian domed hall
used for rock, folk and jazz but especially for classical con-

certs. Famous for the annual Promenade concerts from *Jul-Sep* (see p50). Box office *open 09.00-21.00 Mon-Sun*. A.V.

Royal Festival Hall   **5 A4**
South Bank SE1. 071-928 8800. Built in 1951 for the Festival of Britain, it seats 3000 and hosts mainly choral and orchestral concerts. Box office *open 10.00-20.00 Mon-Sun*. A.Ax.Dc.V.

Wigmore Hall   **4 C2**
36 Wigmore St W1. 071-935 2141. Excellent acoustics and intimate atmosphere. Popular coffee concerts *11.30 Sun*. Stages instrumental, song, chamber music and solo recitals. Seats 540. *Closed for refurbishment at time of publication*. Box office *open 10.00-20.30 Mon-Sun*. A.Ax.Dc.V.

Dinner and entertainment

Dine in elegant surroundings with cabaret entertainment and dancing at one of the following venues. In most cases it is advisable to book in advance.

Barbarella 1   **6 B5**
428 Fulham Rd SW6. 071-385 9434. Cascading fountains, plus a stylish, sophisticated disco. Unusual Italian menu. *D open to 03.00. Closed Sun*. A.Ax.Dc.V. **££**

Entrecôte   **4 F1**
124a Southampton Row WC1. 071-405 1466. Romantic, candlelit atmosphere, with a wide-ranging international menu. Resident dance band plays *from 21.00 Tue-Sat* and a guitarist *early evening & Sun. Open to 23.45, to 22.45 Sun*. A.Ax.Dc.V. **£££**

L'Hirondelle   **4 D3**
199 Swallow St (off Piccadilly) W1. 071-734 1511. Theatre/restaurant with spectacular, glamorous cabaret. International menu. Two groups dance *from 21.30. Open to 03.00. Closed Sun*. Cabaret *23.00 & 01.30*. A.Ax.Dc.V. **£££**

Royal Garden Hotel, Royal Roof Restaurant   **3 C5**
2-24 Kensington High St W8. 071-937 8000. Modern European restaurant with dinner dancing *Sat evening*. Excellent views over Kensington Palace and Gardens. *Open to 22.30, to 23.00 Sat. Closed Sun*. A.Ax.Dc.V. **£££+**

Savoy Restaurant   **4 G3**
Savoy Hotel, Strand WC2. 071-836 4343. Elegant and formal, overlooking the Thames. World-wide and well-deserved reputation. Dancing to the resident quartet. *D open to 23.30. Closed Sun*. A.Ax.Dc.V. **£££+**

Talk of London   **4 F2**
Drury Lane WC2. 071-408 1001. Modern theatre/restaurant featuring some of London's most popular cabaret acts, including music from Andrew Lloyd Webber musicals and other West End hit shows. Dancing to a resident band. French and international cooking. *Open to 24.00*. A.Ax.Dc.V. **£££**

Terrace Restaurant　　　　　　　　　**4 B4**
Dorchester Hotel, Park Lane W1. 071-629 8888. Stately dinner dancing in gracious surroundings. French *haute cuisine. Open to 23.30. Closed Sun & Mon.* A.Ax.Dc.V. **£££**

Terrazza Est　　　　　　　　　　　**5 B2**
109 Fleet St EC4. 071-353 2680. Large basement restaurant known as the Spaghetti Opera for its superb, uplifting opera singing (*from 19.30*). Lively atmosphere. Set and à la carte menus. *Open to 23.00. Closed Sat & Sun.* A.Ax.Dc.V. **££**

Villa dei Cesari　　　　　　　　　　**7 C4**
135 Grosvenor Rd SW1. 071-828 7453. Fine views of the Thames from this converted riverside warehouse themed on the Roman Empire. Classical decor, latinised menu and waiters in tunics. Dancing to resident band. *Open to 02.30. Closed Mon.* A.Ax.Dc.V. **£££+**

Windows on the World, Hilton Hotel　　**4 B4**
Park Lane W1. 071-493 8000. The name is not an exaggeration! Diners are afforded intoxicating views over the city from 28 floors up. Excellent French cooking. Dance floor, two bands. *Open to 01.00.* A.Ax.Dc.V. **£££**

Live music venues

Consult Time Out, What's On *and the music press to check who's playing where, and when.*

Hammersmith Odeon
Queen Caroline St W6. 081-748 4081. Legendary – hosting the full range of bands from major to minor. Usually a good atmosphere. Box office *open 11.00-20.00. Closed Sun.* No credit cards.

100 Club　　　　　　　　　　　　**4 C2**
100 Oxford St W1. 071-636 0933. Friendly and comfortable basement club, historically the home of British traditional jazz. Also modern jazz, blues and swing. *Open to 24.00, to 03.00 Fri, to 01.00 Sat.* No box office. No credit cards.

Marquee　　　　　　　　　　　　**4 E2**
105 Charing Cross Rd WC2. 071-437 6603. One of London's original rock clubs. Still a popular, lively spot. *Open to 24.00, to 03.00 Thur-Sat, to 22.30 Sun.* Box office *open 10.00-18.00 Mon-Fri, 12.00-18.00 Sat.* A.V.

Palookaville　　　　　　　　　　　**4 F3**
13a James St WC2. 071-240 5857. Lively basement restaurant and wine bar in the heart of Covent Garden. Bistro-style food accompanied by traditional or modern jazz. *Open to 01.00. Closed Sun.* A.Ax.Dc.V.

Rock Garden　　　　　　　　　　　**4 F3**
67 Covent Garden Piazza WC2. 071-240 3961. Beneath the restaurant of the same name, a selection of starry-eyed young

bands play in a converted banana warehouse. You might hear tomorrow's stars – U2 and Dire Straits once played here. *Open to 03.00, to 24.00 Sun.* Box office *open from 19.00.* A.V.

Ronnie Scott's 4 E2

47 Frith St W1. 071-439 0747. Reputedly the best jazz club in London. Can be typically hot, smoky and sleazy on a busy night, but it's the sounds people come for. Advisable to book in advance. *Open to 03.00.* Box office *open 11.00-20.00 Mon-Sun.* A.Ax.Dc.V.

Nightclubs and casinos

To join an exclusive clientele in a relaxed and well-tended setting, choose one of the members-only nightclubs. Most of these will provide restaurants and entertainment. Be on your guard, however, for those which also offer 'hostesses' – women employed to boost the sales of drinks. Most of them have an expensive taste in champagne and you will have to pay for the pleasure of their company.

*Most nightclubs will require you to be a member, although short-term membership is usually available for visitors. In some clubs visitors from overseas get reduced rates or free membership. For an annual subscription fee, the **Clubman's Club** 262-264 Albemarle St W1 (071-287 2091) will supply membership and benefits at clubs in Britain and abroad.*

*You can enter a gaming house only as a member or a guest of a member. By law, when you join a gaming club you will not be admitted until you have filled in a declaration of your intent to gamble and 48 hours have elapsed from the time you signed this declaration. The number **(48)** after a club's name means this rule applies.*

(M) *means that membership is necessary for entry.*

Annabel's 4 C3

44 Berkeley Sq W1. 071-629 2350. Legendary haunt of the rich and famous. Past members have included royals, millionaires and showbiz stars. Long waiting list, but you can get a temporary three-week membership if proposed by an existing member. **(M)** *Open to 03.00. Closed Sun.*

Charlie Chester Casino (48) 4 E3

12 Archer St W1. 071-734 0255. Modern, easy-going nightclub with restaurant and gambling rooms. **(M)** *Open to 04.00.*

Clermont Club (48) 4 C3

44 Berkeley Sq W1. 071-493 5587. Opulent 18thC town house, a favourite with London's well-heeled businessmen. A la carte restaurant with Arabic cuisine. **(M)** *Open to 04.00.*

Director's Lodge 4 D4

13 Mason's Yard, Duke St SW1. 071-839 6109. Businessmen's club with hostesses. Restaurant with inter-

national cuisine, resident band. No membership required. *Open to 03.00. Closed Sat & Sun.*

Gaslight of St James's   **4 D4**
4 Duke of York St SW1. 071-930 1648. Two bars, a restaurant and hostesses. **(M)** or entrance fee. *Open to 02.00. Closed Sun.*

Morton's   **4 C3**
28 Berkeley Sq W1. 071-499 0363. Set in a Victorian town house are a late-night disco, bar and restaurant. Attracts wealthy clientele. **(M)**. *Open to 02.00. Closed Sun.*

Stork Club   **4 D3**
99 Regent St W1. 071-734 1393. Luxury restaurant with dance band and spectacular cabaret. **(M)**. *Open to 03.30. Closed Sun.*

Nightspots

These do not require membership and usually host one-night clubs. As fashions change frequently, it's a good idea to phone the venue or consult Time Out *or* What's On *in advance to check what the correct dress is for that night. Entry to most of the following clubs will be **£10.00 or under per person.***

Empire Discotheque   **4 E3**
Leicester Sq WC2. 071-437 1446. Full of lights, mirrors, staircases, balconies and night owls. Diner. Enjoyable and friendly. *Open to 02.00, to 03.30 Thur-Sat.* A.Ax.V.

Hippodrome   **4 E3**
Leicester Sq WC2. 071-437 4311. A black cave of brass and chrome illuminated by an amazing lighting system. Six bars, restaurant. *Open to 03.30. Closed Sun.* A.Ax.Dc.V.

Limelight   **4 E3**
136 Shaftesbury Ave W1. 071-434 0572. Large and lavish club, housed somewhat incongruously in a former Welsh Presbyterian Church. Very popular at weekends. Excellent restaurant. *Open to 03.30. Closed Sun.* A.Ax.Dc.V.

Le Palais
242 Shepherd's Bush Rd W6. 081-748 2812. Very popular mainstream discotheque with glitzy, art-deco furnishing, a restaurant, and a laser show. *Open to 02.00 Wed & Thur, to 03.00 Fri & Sat. Closed Sun.* A.Ax.Dc.V.

Stringfellows   **4 F3**
16 Upper St Martin's Lane WC2. 071-240 5534. Most celebrities have been photographed flashing their teeth and jewellery at Stringfellows, but beware – the rich and famous tend to keep themselves to themselves. A la carte restaurant. *Open to 03.30. Closed Sun.* A.Ax.Dc.V.

The Wag   **4 E3**
35 Wardour St W1. 071-437 5534. Attracts an exuberant, young clientele. Weekend nights are very popular. *Open to 03.30, to 06.00 Fri & Sat. Closed Sun.* No credit cards.

EMERGENCY INFORMATION & SERVICES

ACCIDENT/AMBULANCE
If there's an accident or you need an ambulance for any reason, dial **999** and ask for ambulance.

BABYSITTING AND CHILDCARE
Chelsea Baby Hire
081-870 5846. Do not hire babies, as you might think, but everything else: push-chairs, children's seats, cots etc from one night onwards. Phone enquiries only. Free delivery and collection service within central London.

Universal Aunts   6 E3
250 King's Rd SW3. 071-371 9766. Comprehensive service offering babysitters, cooks, proxy parents, someone to prepare parties etc.

CAR BREAKDOWN
AA (Automobile Association)
Freephone breakdown service 0800 887766. *24hrs Mon-Sun.* You can call the AA out if your car breaks down, but you will have to join on the spot if you are not already a member. A.V.

National Breakdown
Freephone breakdown service 0800 400600. *24hrs Mon-Sun.* Non-members will pay more for rescue/recovery than members. A.V.

Olympic Breakdown Service
071-286 8282. *24hrs Mon-Sun.* An AA- and RAC-approved recovery service covering the whole of London. A.Ax.V.

RAC (Royal Automobile Club)
Freephone breakdown service 0800 828282. *24hrs Mon-Sun.* You will need to be a member of the RAC, or join when they arrive. A.Ax.V.

CHEMISTS (Late night)
The local police station keeps a list of chemists and doctors available at all hours.

Bliss Chemist   3 G3
5 Marble Arch W1. 071-723 6116. *Open 09.00-24.00 every*

day of the year. Also at 50-56 Willesden Lane NW6. 071-624
8000. *Open 09.00-24.00 Mon-Sun.*

Boots   **4 E3**
Piccadilly Circus W1. 071-734 6126. *Open 08.30-20.00 Mon-
Fri, 09.00-20.00 Sat, 12.00-18.00 Sun.* Also at 75 Queensway
W2 071-229 9266. *Open 09.00-22.00 Mon-Sat.*

Warman Freed
45 Golders Green Rd NW11. 081-455 4351. *Open 08.00-24.00
every day of the year.*

CREDIT CARDS
*If you have lost an **Access** or **Visa** card issued by a bank in the
UK, contact the emergency number of the issuing bank:*
Barclays
(0604) 230230. *24hrs.*
Lloyds
(0702) 362988. *24hrs.*
Midland
081-450 3122. *24hrs.*
National Westminster
(0532) 778899. *24hrs.*
Royal Bank of Scotland
(0702) 362988. *24hrs.*

*Contact the emergency numbers listed below if you have lost
the following cards:*
American Express
(0273) 696933. *24hrs.*
Diners Club
(0252) 516261. *24hrs.*
Eurocheque card
(0532) 778899. *24hrs.*

*If you have lost a **Visa** or **Mastercard** issued abroad, contact
the following:*
Mastercard
(0702) 362988. *24hrs.*
Visa
(0604) 230230. *24hrs.*

HOSPITALS
Free medical treatment is available under the National Health
Service (NHS) to British citizens, students studying courses of
six months or more, people who are working in Britain, EC
Nationals and visitors from other countries with reciprocal
arrangements. **All** other foreign visitors will be required to pay
for medical treatment they receive.
24-hour hospital casualty departments
Charing Cross Hospital
Fulham Palace Rd, Hammersmith W6. 081-846 1234.

Guy's Hospital   **5 E4**
St Thomas St SE1. 071-955 5000.
Hammersmith Hospital
Du Cane Rd, Shepherd's Bush W12. 081-743 2030.
London Hospital
Whitechapel Rd, Whitechapel E1. 071-377 7000.
Royal Free Hospital
Pond St, Hampstead NW3. 071-794 0500.
St Bartholomew's Hospital   **5 C1**
West Smithfield EC1. 071-601 8888.
St Thomas's Hospital   **4 G6**
Lambeth Palace Rd SE1. 071-928 9292.
University College Hospital   **1 F5**
Gower St WC1. 071-387 9300.
Westminster Hospital   **7 E2**
Dean Ryle St, Horseferry Rd SW1. 081-746 8000.
Whittington Hospital
Highgate Hill, Archway N19. 071-272 3070.

LATE-NIGHT FOOD
Burger King   **4 E3**
17-21 Leicester Sq WC2. No phone. Member of the well-known chain. Burgers, fries and milkshakes. *Open to 04.30, to 02.00 Sun.*
Harry's   **4 D3**
19 Kingly St W1. 071-434 0309. A nightclubbers' institution. Late-night breakfasts and lively atmosphere. *Open to 06.30.*
Lido   **4 E3**
41 Gerrard St W1. 071-437 4437. Busy and friendly Chinese restaurant. *Open to 04.00.*
Up All Night   **6 C4**
325 Fulham Rd SW10. 071-352 1996. Steaks, burgers and spaghetti served by lively staff. *Open to 06.00. Closed Sun.*

LATE POST
Most post offices close at 17.30 *Mon-Fri &* 12.00 *Sat. However, there is one late opening office in London:*
Post Office   **4 F3**
24-28 William IV St, Trafalgar Sq WC2. 071-930 9580. *Open 08.00-20.00 Mon-Sat.*

LOST PROPERTY
Airports
For property lost in the main airport buildings phone the British Airport Authorities Lost Property Office, Heathrow Airport, Middx. 081-759 4321. Or contact the airport direct (see p18) for a list of airports.
British Rail (trains)
If you lose something on a train, contact the station where the

train you were on terminates. They will be able to inform you whether your belongings have been recovered, and if so, where they have been taken. See p22 for the list of London British Rail stations.

London Transport (tubes)   1 B5
Lost Property Office, 200 Baker St W1 (next to Baker St Station). For enquiries about lost property please call in person (or send another person with written authority) or apply by letter. No telephone enquiries. *Open 09.30-14.00 Mon-Fri. Closed Bank hols.*

Taxis
If you leave anything in a taxi, phone the Metropolitan Police Lost Property Office 071-833 0996. *Open 09.00-16.00 Mon-Fri.*

Passports
Report the loss to the police and to your embassy/high commission.

PUBLIC LAVATORIES
Look out for signs in the street directing you to the nearest public lavatory, or ask someone likely to be familiar with the area; police, traffic wardens, news-vendors and shop-keepers. All public lavatories are divided into separate areas for men and women except the newer cabin-style ones which are found in the street. These are completely self-contained and therefore unisex. They are *open 24hrs* and you will need exactly the right coins to use them. Nearly all large department stores, museums and national art galleries have lavatories, as do pubs, mainline British Rail stations and several of the central London parks. NB: There are no public lavatories on Underground trains, nor in most Underground stations.

WHEELCLAMPED
If you get wheelclamped, take the label attached to your vehicle, plus the fixed penalty notice, to one of the police car pounds listed below. You will have to pay a (high) fine before the clamp is removed. (A.Ax.Dc.V.). It can be some time before someone arrives to remove it, but you must return to and stay with your car. In an emergency telephone 071-252 2222. If you are causing an obstruction your car may be towed away to one of the following pounds. Fines for recovery are very high.

Camden Town Car Pound   1 D2
Oval Rd NW1. *Open 08.00-24.00 Mon-Sat.*

Hyde Park Car Pound   4 B4
NCP Park Lane Car Park, Marble Arch W1. *Open 24hrs.*

Mount Pleasant Car Pound   2 B5
cnr of Calthorpe St & Farringdon Rd EC1. *Open 08.00-24.00.*

Warwick Road Car Pound
245 Warwick Rd, West Kensington W14. *Open 08.00-24.00 Mon-Sat.*